DATE DUE

WOMEN'S WORK
IN BRITAIN AND AMERICA
from the Nineties to World War I

an annotated bibliography

A
Reference
Publication
in
Women's Studies

Barbara Haber
Editor

WOMEN'S WORK
IN BRITAIN AND AMERICA
from the Nineties to World War I

an annotated bibliography

MARY DRAKE McFEELY

G.K.HALL &CO.

70 LINCOLN STREET, BOSTON, MASS.

HD
6135
.M33X

Library of Congress Cataloging in Publication Data

McFeely, Mary Drake.
  Women's work in Britain and America.

  Bibliography
  Includes indexes.
    1. Women—Employment—Great Britain—Bibliography.
  2. Women—Employment—United States—Bibliography.
  3. Women volunteers in social service—Great Britain—
  Bibliography. 4. Women volunteers in social service—
  United States—Bibliography. I. Title.
  Z7963.E7M43 1982 [HD6135] 016.3314'0941   82-9281
  ISBN 0-8161-8504-2   AACR2

This publication is printed on permanent/durable acid-free paper
MANUFACTURED IN THE UNITED STATES OF AMERICA

For Bill

Contents

The Author

Mary Drake McFeely is Head Reference Librarian at Smith College. A regular reviewer for Library Journal, she was a member of the biography jury for the American Book Awards in 1981. She spent the year 1978-79 in England doing research for this book on a fellowship from the Council on Library Resources.

Preface

This bibliography is intended to assist and stimulate research on British and American women's work during the period 1890 to 1914. I hope that it will be useful to scholars and students who are interested in women's activities and, more generally, in the economic and social history of the period, as well as in the comparative history of the two societies.

SCOPE

Work is defined broadly to include both paid employment and unpaid work in social welfare and other pursuits. The bibliography includes books (fiction and nonfiction), pamphlets, and articles written between 1890 and 1914 and material written later that deals with the period. I have not considered works published later than December 1980. Unpublished works are beyond the scope of this book, although guides to manuscript collections and archives have been included. I have examined all the publications listed, and have selected them from among the many items that exist. Entries are included because of the factual information they contain, the point of view they represent, or the interpretive analysis they provide. In some cases, I have included the best or only material available in hopes that a researcher may be inspired to improve upon it.

The history of women and trade unions is, of course, an important aspect of this topic. Martha Jane Soltow and Mary K. Wery's bibliography, American Women and the Labor Movement 1825-1974 (entry 509), so thoroughly covers this subject as it applies to the United States that I have not attempted to go over the same ground. Instead, in dealing with the United States I have concentrated on subjects that fall outside the scope of their work, such as domestic servants, professional women, and philanthropists, and on works published since 1974.

Since material on women's work appears in such a wide variety of publications, researchers will undoubtedly come across additional material; I will be happy to hear of such discoveries.

Preface

METHODOLOGY

Major bibliographies consulted in preparation of this book include the London Bibliography of the Social Sciences (London: London School of Economics, 1931-32) and its supplements; H. J. Hanham, Bibliography of British History 1851-1914 (Oxford: Clarendon Press, 1976); and the published catalogues of the Arthur and Elizabeth Schlesinger Library on the History of Women in America, Radcliffe College, Cambridge, Massachusetts and the Sophia Smith Collection, Smith College, Northampton, Massachusetts (entries 332a and 509a). The Fiction Catalog, 1st ed. (New York: H. W. Wilson, 1908); the Nineteenth Century Readers' Guide to Periodical Literature; the Readers' Guide to Periodical Literature; and the International Index to Periodicals were useful in finding material written during the period. Continuing bibliographic guides to historical writings that I used include America: History and Life, Historical Abstracts, and Writings in American History. Bibliographic notes in issues of History Workshop Journal, Labor History, and the Bulletin of the Society for the Study of Labour History brought to my attention recent work, sometimes published in regional journals, that I might otherwise have missed.

Much of the research for this book was done in the British Library, the British Library of Political and Economic Science, the Fawcett Collection at the City of London Polytechnic, the Institute for Historical Research at the University of London, the library of University College, London, and the University of London Library. In the United States I have used the Smith College Library and the Arthur and Elizabeth Schlesinger Collection, as well as many other resources through interlibrary loans.

ARRANGEMENT

The bibliography is arranged in two sections: Women's Work in Great Britain and Women's Work in America. Entries in each section are in alphabetical order by author (by personal name or name of institution), or by title if no author has been cited. Access to particular items is available through author, title, and subject indexes; index numbers refer to entry numbers, not pages. In using the indexes it will be helpful to remember that entries numbered 1 through 319 are in the section on Great Britain, while those numbered 320 on refer to the section on the United States. Because there were very few comparative works, I have not listed them in a separate section, but included them under one or the other country; they are indexed under topical subject headings with the subheading "comparative study."

Preface

FORM OF ENTRY

Form of entry follows the standard of the University of Chicago Press, A Manual of Style, 12th ed., revised (1969). Abbreviations are the customary ones, such as n.d., where no date of publication is available, or n.p., where no publisher is given. Some periodical references give volume numbers as o.s. (old series) or n.s. (new series). Items described as "available from EDRS" are published by the United States Office of Education in microfiche or hard copy. When a book or article includes a substantial or especially useful bibliography, I have mentioned it in the annotation.

ACKNOWLEDGMENTS

I am grateful for a Council on Library Resources fellowship and a research leave from Smith College that combined to allow me to devote a year of uninterrupted time to this bibliography. The Smith College Library's strong collection of books on women stimulated my interest in the subject. Encouraged by what I found there, I read in other libraries in the United States and in England. Everywhere I worked, librarians were most helpful. I wish particularly to thank the staff members of the Fawcett Collection, who supplied advice as well as access to that remarkable collection of material on women in England. Through the Women's Research and Resources Centre in London I met scholars working in the field.

Many people have been generous with advice and suggestions. Mark Aldrich, Michael Burns, Peter Clarke, Anna Davin, Maureen Ritchie, Raphael Samuel, Pat Thane, and Charles Trout deserve special thanks. My husband, William S. McFeely, and my children, Drake, Eliza, and Jennifer McFeely have supplied both encouragement and practical help that made it possible for me to persevere.

Introduction

Women in Britain and in America in the 1890s and in the early years of the twentieth century showed an increasing awareness of their abilities and their responsibilities. With a new consciousness that the future could not be left to take care of itself, they realized that they could and should bring about change. Women went to work redefining the way women work.

Work is, of course, a complicated concept, and I have defined the term broadly. Women earned wages, but they also did unpaid jobs in households and on farms. Many labored seriously and consistently without pay in settlements, social investigation, and philanthropy. Women pressed for access to the professions, but they also turned their attention to social welfare. As their numbers at work in factories, shops, and offices increased, broad questions emerged about working conditions, wages, and women's traditional occupation, the family. "Women's work," therefore, includes all of these.

The First World War is frequently seen as a time of great breakthroughs when many women were called to work, but the real changes had begun earlier. Looking back from our perspective in the twentieth century, we can see that women's consciousness of themselves as individuals and of their economic and social needs appears to have been a cohesive force in the last decade of the nineteenth century. This awareness solidified into organization and action during the period before the war.

The range of women's occupations broadened in the United Kingdom and in the United States. While the percentage employed in industry remained stable, the percentage employed as servants decreased, and women entered clerical occupations in rapidly increasing numbers. (In the United States, the percentage of employed women who took office or business-related jobs rose from 5.3% in 1890 to 14.8% in 1910.) They became telephone operators, saleswomen, and clerks. The number of educated women who became teachers greatly increased, but many also turned to the newer professions such as trained nursing, librarianship, and social work. In 1893, the year that Florence Kelley was appointed chief factory inspector in Illinois, May Abraham and Mary Paterson became the first women factory inspectors in England. In 1911 Hilda Martindale reported that she had traveled ten thousand miles as a factory inspector in Ireland; by 1914 there were twenty-one lady factory inspectors in England.

The United States population remained predominantly rural until after World War I, and although Britain's urbanization occurred earlier, a substantial part of the population still lived in the country. The literature emphasizes the activities of urban women, but rural women were working on farms and pursuing crafts such as needlework and straw plaiting, and some, like Elizabeth Watris Pringle (entry 488), were managing their own plantations or farms. The United States Department of Agriculture's survey of farm women collected letters that described both the hardships and the pleasures of life on remote farms (entry 525).

In 1890 most trade unions excluded women. By 1914 some women had entered existing unions, although their welcome was seldom enthusiastic. Others, often with the assistance of the Women's Trade Union League, organized their own.

Increased access to higher education produced a group of women with a keen sense of social responsibility and an interest in the welfare of other women. They emerged from Girton or Newnham in Britain, or from Smith, Vassar, or the University of Wisconsin in America, convinced of their duty to do something socially useful. They became active in the United States in social settlements, in union organizing, and in movements for protective legislation for women and children, as well as in suffrage movements on both sides of the Atlantic.

As women entered occupations formerly reserved for men in offices and in professions such as journalism, as well as in printing and other industries where mechanization reduced the requirements of physical strength, the previously accepted notion of the male as sole breadwinner came into question, and people argued about the right of women to compete in the job market. Although many women (as well as men) found it hard to think of themselves as permanent members of the work force, social investigators discovered that in fact, a substantial number of women were the chief support for themselves and others.

More worked at domestic service than at any other paid employment, even though the proportion of working women in this occupation decreased. Beginning work at a very early age, sometimes as the only servant in the household, sometimes as part of a large staff, the woman or girl was isolated in either case by the long hours and strict rules that prevailed. The employer determined working conditions, which consequently varied greatly. There was a vague but widely held conviction that domestic service gave young girls an opportunity to learn the skills of housekeeping, but this was countered by the argument that in learning the domestic ways of the middle class, girls were spoiled for married life with members of their own class.

Servants were not successfully brought into trade unions because of their isolation in individual households. Without organization, they lacked protection against unemployment or inability to work because of poor health or old age, and many ended a life of diligent work in poverty.

It is not surprising that as work opportunities in shops and factories increased, fewer girls chose domestic service. The so-called servant problem became an issue much discussed in middle-class journals such as the Nineteenth Century. Proposals appeared for ways to make servant life more attractive; Lady Aberdeen in 1892 described a servants' club in a large household (presumably her own) that offered group activities and drawing classes as well as lectures given by the master's houseguests (entry 2). Charlotte Perkins Gilman's 1898 proposal for centralization and professionalization of housework and meal preparation (entry 407) was widely discussed, if little practiced, on both sides of the Atlantic. The Women's Industrial Council in London obtained responses from both employers and servants to a questionnaire concerning attitudes toward conditions of domestic service. Only a few memoirs of former servants are available, often written decades after the experience, but two British autobiographies, Louise Jermy's Memories of a Working Woman (entry 153) and Hannah Mitchell's The Hard Way Up (entry 207), give insight into this occupation with its unusual degree of personal involvement between employee and employer.

Recent historians have used the available sources in interesting ways to speculate on "life below stairs." Pamela Horn's 1975 study, The Rise and Fall of the Victorian Servant (entry 141), reviews the structure, hierarchy, duties, and social situation of various sizes of English households, carefully producing a well-balanced picture of servants and masters. Theresa M. McBride (entry 180) asks imaginative questions of the available information and discusses the effects of the relationship on both employer and employee in England and France. Leonore Davidoff ("Mastered for Life," entry 65) compares the subordinate positions of servants and wives in Victorian and Edwardian England. David M. Katzman's Seven Days a Week (entry 433) perceptively analyzes the problems and conditions of domestic service in the United States, with attention to the changing racial and ethnic factors that make the picture so different from the English one.

The English governess was among the most isolated of women. As a servant she was beneath association with the family in whose household she lived, but the servants shunned her as a member of the middle class. Becoming a governess was the fate of many a female who was not provided for by a father, brother, or husband, as illustrated by the heroines of the abundant literature, the best known examples of which are Jane Eyre and Daniel Deronda.

Among the efforts to expand the employment possibilities of un-
trained middle-class English women was the idea of "lady helps."
Essentially, the concept was that of a refined housekeeper, but low
esteem for any work performed in someone else's house prevented wide
acceptance of this as an honorable occupation. Alice Zimmern (entry
319) and M. Mostyn Bird (entry 15) in England, Grace Hoadley Dodge
(entry 381) in the United States, and others compiled dictionaries
of employment to suggest a wide range of other possibilities, from
landscape gardening to goldfish farming. Queen Mary, herself a
skilled needleworker, led efforts to encourage women proficient in
this art to sell their work; in the United States the Women's Exchange
started as an outlet for women's crafts.

The great increase in retail stores and ready-made clothing
opened a new field for women in the late nineteenth century. As
sales clerks (in the United States) or shop assistants (in England)
they shared with servants the handicap of the employer's total control of their lives; shop hours were long, and even well-intentioned
employers thought they must keep the same hours as their competition.
In England, living-in, an arrangement whereby shop assistants shared
living accommodations provided by the employer, was usual; rules in
these establishments, as in the shops, were strict, ostensibly to
keep the young clerks from falling into wicked ways. The threat of
losing room and board as well as wages in the event of dismissal kept
the employees on their toes. Despite these similarities to the conditions of domestic service, retail selling enjoyed a higher social
status than service or factory work. In the United States, the number of saleswomen went from 7,462 in 1880 to 100,000 in 1890, and
228,000 in 1900. In The Lower Middle Class in England 1870-1914
(entry 60), Geoffrey Crossick offers an interesting analysis of people whose work was service to the middle and upper classes, who must
imitate the customers' dress and behavior but still "know their place."

Efforts to improve the working conditions of clerks began before
the turn of the century in both countries. In England, Margaret
Bondfield, a union organizer and political activist, organized the
National Union of Shop Assistants, and argued for the right to sit
down while on duty (an issue that was debated in the House of Lords).
In the United States, Josephine Shaw Lowell, a philanthropist, started
the Consumers' League of New York, which campaigned to persuade shoppers to patronize only those stores in which working conditions met
certain standards and to purchase only goods made under decent conditions. Philanthropists also organized clubs, such as the Girls'
Friendly Society in England, to provide companionship and recreation
for young working girls.

Margaret Bondfield wrote several articles on the working conditions of shop assistants; her own experiences in such a job are described in Mary Agnes Hamilton's biography (entry 114). Hannah
Mitchell's autobiography (entry 207) tells of her work in shops.
Except in general studies of women's work, however, historians have

given little attention to this occupation. It would be illuminating, for example, to know what people went on to do when they left selling, for in 1900 the average age of clerks was 22.

Invention of the typewriter and the development of large clerical staffs for business and government offices opened a new area of work for women. After an initial period of suspicion as to the propriety of office work (one London concern whose business was clerical services had their women "typewriters" on display in a store window so passersby could see how respectable they were, and so other young women might be attracted to the work) it became a popular occupation. By 1900, 212,000 women in the United States were engaged in this kind of work. Efforts to unionize typists and stenographers began as early as 1882, but many considered themselves too genteel to join a union.

By 1890, women were well established in manufacturing. They generally occupied the bottom rung of unskilled jobs, as employers found them not only willing to work for much less pay, but docile and less likely than men to make trouble or to organize. In most industries, the men who held skilled jobs saw to it that women had no opportunity to learn such work. There were exceptions, however, as in both countries women textile workers were numerous, outspoken, and strong. Many women factory workers were young and planned to leave the factory when they married, but in the meanwhile they enjoyed the companionship of their fellow workers. Thus the high visibility of the cheeky, gaudily dressed "factory girls" fostered a generally accepted belief that women in industry were only working for pocket money, a concept social reformers found hard to dispel.

From the 1890s on, both reformers and government inspectors peered into the factory and reported on the conditions for women workers. The report on a 1906 Birmingham survey (entry 45) is an English example, comparable to Elizabeth Beardsley Butler's 1911 study of Pittsburgh (entry 363). Annual reports of the Lady Factory Inspectors form an extensive source for England from 1896 onward. The massive Report on Condition of Woman and Child Wage Earners in the United States (entry 524), prepared by the Bureau of Labor and published as a Senate Document in 1911, provides a detailed survey. Novelists such as Sabine Baring-Gould (entry 8) drew attention to the dangers of work in the potteries and elsewhere. Edith Sophie Lyttelton's play (entry 177) dramatized the plight of overworked dressmakers at the height of the London season.

Not all women manufacturing workers did their tasks inside the factory. In 1906 the London Daily News sponsored an Exhibition of Sweated Industries to rouse public attention to the conditions under which home-workers labored and the miserable wages they earned. The exhibition not only supplied factual information about manufacture of articles under the sweating system, but displayed workers performing their jobs; visitors were reminded that the workers were not allowed to accept money while on exhibit. Edith F. Hogg, an active member of

Introduction

the Women's Trade Union Association and the Women's Industrial Council, described the women who prepared rabbit skins for hats (entry 135). In the United States, Mary Van Kleeck, beginning a long career of industrial investigation, did a series of Russell Sage Foundation reports on home-workers (entries 526-528), including artificial flower-makers and bookbinders, that helped to promote legislation prohibiting home-work. Novels like Comrade Yetta (entry 360) and Children of Gibeon (entry 13) poignantly described the hard, life-shortening work of sweated laborers.

Some people argued that legislating home-work out of existence would deprive the workers of their only means of earning even a tiny wage. When Mary Macarthur caught diphtheria from a woman she visited in the course of her investigation of home-work in London for the Anti-Sweating League, her brush with death was her strongest argument when she sought legislation. Similarly, in the United States the Consumers' League pressed middle-class shoppers to the realization that articles manufactured in crowded tenements and sweatshops carried disease into their own households.

In the United States in the late nineteenth century new women's colleges such as Bryn Mawr and Vassar, and coordinate colleges like Barnard were founded and the number of universities open to women increased. In 1890 56,000 women were enrolled in institutions of higher learning, and by 1910 that number had risen to 140,000. In England women were admitted to University College London; they were permitted to study, but not until much later to take degrees, at Oxford and Cambridge. Many of these educated women looked about for ways to make their learning socially useful.

Teaching had long been an occupation to which working-class girls could aspire and Oxford-educated women had recourse, as the heroine of Emma Brooke's 1895 novel, Transition (entry 40), learned. In 1907 the requirement of a college education for teacher certification was established in England; this helped to promote a standard of competence, but it closed the profession to many working-class women who could not afford to put off earning a living until they were twenty-one in order to go to college. In the same year, Indiana became the first state to require its teachers to have a high-school education.

Nursing was a profession struggling for respectability. Working-class nurses had long had a reputation for heavy drinking and promiscuity; the educated women who established training schools for nurses attempted to counteract this with a code of behavior that was convent-like in its strictness. Nevertheless, after teaching, nursing became the largest profession for women, accounting for 76,000 American women in 1910, and 78,000 English women in 1911. The attempt to set standards and establish a licensing or registry system that would lend status and reliability to nursing and midwifery encountered obstacles set up by doctors who preferred not to compete with professional women whose fees were lower than their own. The Nurses' Registration Act,

Introduction

first presented to Parliament in 1909, was not passed until 1919.
The licensing of midwives turned out to be so restrictive that in
the United States the profession all but disappeared, while in England their number was greatly reduced. In Midwives and Medical Men
(entry 77), Jean Donnison analyzes the rivalries and political bat-
tles on this question in England; Judy Barrett Litoff (entry 457)
does the same for the United States.

Interestingly, women who themselves had fought for entry into the
medical profession opposed the licensing of midwives. They objected
to partial medical training that led to a lesser profession--women in
medicine should be doctors or nothing. Gains were made in opening
medical training to women with the establishment of the Women's
Medical College of Pennsylvania in 1850, the New Hospital for Women
(now the Elizabeth Garrett Anderson Hospital) in London in 1866, and
the London School of Medicine for women in 1874. In 1902, Emily
Dunning Barringer became the first woman intern in a New York City
hospital.

Entry into the legal profession was still more difficult. As
late as 1911, a male solicitor gently proposed in the pages of
Englishwoman that women lawyers would do no harm (entry 225).

Women who were trained scientists found it difficult to break
into academia except in women's colleges like Mount Holyoke. They
found employment as researchers in expanding government agencies such
as the United States Department of Agriculture and as research assistants in astronomy. Under the vigorous leadership of Ellen Swallow
Richards, home economics emerged as a teaching and research field
for American women scientists. Margaret W. Rossiter (entries 493
and 494) outlined the work of women scientists before 1920 and
suggested possibilities for futher work.

Family responsibilities or the social restrictions surrounding
the middle and upper classes prevented some women from establishing
a career; instead, philanthropic or reform work took the place of a
profession. New organizations aimed at investigating or ameliorating
social problems proliferated. The Women's Industrial Council, for
example, was founded in London in 1894. Among its activities were
investigations of the pay, hours, and working conditions of nurses,
of occupations of girls leaving elementary schools, and of swimming
accommodations for working women in London. The Council responded
to its findings by organizing clubs and lending libraries for working
girls, and implementing training programs to improve the chances for
employment of unskilled women. Mrs. Pember Reeves set out on behalf
of another organization, the Fabian Women's Group, to study the effect
of maternal nutrition on babies in East London, and became fascinated
with the problems of women who managed the family's needs on an income
of "round about a pound a week" (entry 242). Under the leadership of
Florence Kelley, the National Consumers' League, founded by Maude
Nathan and Josephine Shaw Lowell, became an important pressure group

in Chicago, Boston, and New York, recommending products and stores on
the basis of working conditions and environments. The energies and
organizational skills of educated women launched the Women's Trade
Union Leagues in both countries. Middle-class and working-class
women met in the risky arena of these organizations. Sometimes they
worked well together; often, however, the working women resented the
interference with its intimations of moral improvement, or they were
too tired and beset with daily cares to join in a common effort with
long-term goals. In To the Lighthouse, Virginia Woolf describes
Mrs. Ramsay, visiting

> this widow, or that struggling wife in person with a bag
> under her arm, and a note-book and pencil with which she
> wrote down in columns carefully ruled for the purpose
> wages and spendings, employment and unemployment, in the
> hope that thus she would cease to be a private woman
> whose charity was half a sop to her own indignation, half
> a relief to her own curiosity, and become, what with her
> untrained mind she greatly admired, an investigator,
> eludicating the social problem.*

The originators did learn from the experience. What began as
philanthropy developed for some into a career. Those who worked with
the poor in settlement houses and other organizations began to feel
the need for training, and the profession of social work took shape.

Some women investigated on their own. Bessie and Marie Van Vorst,
sisters-in-law from New York, left their comfortable home and found
jobs in factories in the eastern United States, sharing the hard work,
the lack of security, and the fun of the factory girls, and writing
about it for their own social peers (entry 529). Mary Higgs
(entries 131 and 132) disguised herself as a tramp to find out what
lodgings for women vagrants in England were like.

Settlement work drew many college graduates to the city slums.
For some of them, like Jane Addams and Florence Kelley in Chicago,
this was an early step in a career of political reform. After gradu-
ating from Bryn Mawr and doing graduate work at Barnard, Josephine
Goldmark became active in research on the legal defense of labor laws.
She worked with her brother-in-law to write the famous Brandeis
briefs supporting legislation limiting hours of work (entry 410).

These organizations and the interaction of women across class
lines have received little attention from historians. The reports
they wrote, their memoirs, and autobiographies have a double interest
for what they relate and for what they reveal about their authors.
Magdalen Stuart Reeves's Round About a Pound a Week (entry 242),

---

*Virginia Woolf, To the Lighthouse (London: The Hogarth Press,
1977), pp. 19-20.

Introduction

articles in the Economic Journal by Clementina Black, Bessie and
Marie Van Vorst's American The Woman Who Toils (entry 529), and the
Russell Sage reports, are examples. Jim Leonard's 1975 article on
Lady Bell and her study of the factory workers of Middlesbrough
(entry 169) is an interesting evaluation of the early social investigations using present-day standards. Allen F. Davis's Spearheads for
Reform (entry 378) deals with settlement work in the United States.
The history of organizations like the Women's Industrial Council and
the Consumers' League, the Metropolitan Association for Befriending
Young Servants, and the Association of Trained Charwomen, their mem-
berships (frequently overlapping), and elaboration of their impact
could further illuminate the social concerns of these women. Comparative studies of the organizations might also be fruitful.

As women came to work at a greater variety of occupations and in
increasing numbers, controversies arose over related issues. Surveys,
political pamphlets, and journal articles show a decided diversity of
opinion: Was protective legislation for women workers a necessity or
an unfair handicap? Should sweated labor be abolished by law, or was
it cruel to snatch away the workers' only (if pitifully meager) means
of support? Was it fair to have a wage differential that assumed that
a man supported a family but a woman only worked for pin money? Could
women's competitive positions in the job market be improved by technical training and vocational guidance, encouraging them to work in a
wider range of occupations? If mothers worked, were they giving their
children a better chance in life by increasing the family income, or
dooming them to ill health, early death, or a life of crime by care-
less housekeeping and lack of moral discipline? If the latter, should
the state support them through endowment of motherhood to ensure a
future supply of good citizens and soldiers? Debates on these subjects appear throughout the publications of the period. Recent studies such as Anna Davin's "Imperialism and Motherhood" (entry 71) and
Carol Dyhouse's "Working-Class Mothers and Infant Mortality" (entry
79) show the relationship between these arguments and the intellectual and political setting in which they took place. Both authors
suggest that they are only beginning the exploration of this
relationship.

Arguments for and against factory legislation to protect women
workers against hazardous conditions in the workplace and exploitation through ever-increasing hours and decreasing wages were debated
vigorously. American reformers such as Josephine Goldmark and Mary
Van Kleeck vigorously supported legislative action to limit hours of
work and control the safety of working conditions. E. Jessie
Boucherett and Helen Blackburn (The Condition of Working Women and
the Factory Acts, entry 36) contended that in Britain such legislation unjustly deprived women of the opportunity to work; individuals
should determine the hours they were willing to work, and employers
should be required to correct hazardous conditions rather than prevent women from performing their jobs where dangers exist. Amy
Harrison (Women's Industries in Liverpool, entry 123), B. Leigh

Introduction

Hutchins and Amy Harrison (A History of Factory Legislation, entry 148), and James Ramsay Macdonald (Women in the Printing Trades, entry 184) were among those who reviewed the situation and found that protective legislation had cost few women their jobs. To people of this persuasion, the low rate of participation of women in trade unions and their lack of political power proved that women needed the protection of the state. Similarly, the recollections of English women factory inspectors charged with enforcing the Factory Acts (Rose Squire, Hilda Martindale, and Adelaide Anderson) are unanimous in their conviction that even when protected by law, women hesitated to make complaints for fear of losing their jobs. Since the question of protective legislation continues to be controversial today, the arguments and the actual effects of the laws merit study. For instance, James A. Schmiechen shows in a 1975 study (entry 260) that in London, far from favoring larger, more centralized, and better organized factories, the Factory Acts encouraged smaller operations that could be moved frequently and easily to escape the eye of the inspectors. Thus workers, seeing the social disorganization produced by state legislation, became more aware of the importance of their own organization and political action.

Those who opposed protective legislation advocated developing women's political power through trade union organization. Women cigarmakers in England organized their own union in 1887, and it was amalgamated with the men's union in 1895. The Women's Ropemakers' Union organized a strike in 1890. In the United States, during the depression years of 1893-94, Mary Kenney, who had learned labor-organizing in Chicago, and John F. O'Sullivan (whom she married in 1894) organized some forty unions for women.

Yet for the most part, the organization of women workers made very slow progress. Most male union leaders did their best to keep women out and used the union's strength to prevent employment of women except in unskilled jobs. Many women were reluctant to join the union even when the opportunity existed. The Women's Trade Union League led the effort to organize women. In England the Women's Protective and Provident League was founded in 1875; it became the Women's Provident League and, in 1891, the Women's Trade Union League. In 1903, Mary Kenney O'Sullivan and William English Walling, the settlement worker from New York, brought the idea to the United States using the British organization as a model. Usually, the League went into a factory at a critical moment when wages had been lowered or someone had been unfairly fired, seized the moment, organized a union, conducted a successful action, and then tried to keep the union going. Frequently, when the crisis was over, the women dropped out; but Shela Lewenhak (entry 170) contends that women's low interest in unions occurred in periods when, because of economic conditions and employer pressure, men were inactive too.

Leaders of the women's trade union movement increasingly believed that solidarity with the men was the best policy, but even when women

joined men they failed to participate in union committee work or hold
office. The reasons are still being debated.

Barbara Drake's Women in Trade Unions (entry 78) remains the
basic work on British unions, concentrating on politics, while
Lewenhak gives more attention to people who were important in the
movement. Lucy Middleton, editor of Women in the Labour Movement
(entry 206) emphasizes the relationship of women with the Labour
party. Jill Liddington and Jill Norris (One Hand Tied Behind Us,
entry 172) studied Lancashire women, mostly textile workers, showing
how the political experience gained in the unions was used when they
became active suffragists. Philip S. Foner has written a comprehensive history of women in the American labor movement (entry 401) and
Soltow and Wery's bibliography (entry 509) is a thorough guide to the
literature from 1825 to 1974. Barbara Mayer Wertheimer (We Were
There, entry 537) includes interesting material on American trade
unions. Robin Miller Jacoby's "Feminism and Class Consciousness in
the British and American Women's Trade Union Leagues, 1890-1925"
(entry 431) is an excellent comparative study.

Modern studies of the organization of women in specific trades
are scarce. Histories such as William Henry Warburton's History of
Trade Union Organization in the North Staffordshire Potteries (entry
287) or Norman H. Cuthbert's The Lace Makers Society (entry 62) gave
little attention to women workers, who were restricted to certain
kinds of work in both industries. The mutual education of women industrial workers and the Women's Trade Union League activists warrants
further exploration. Leaders such as Mary Macarthur and Margaret
Bondfield in England and Mary Kenney O'Sullivan in the United States
deserve serious biographical study.

Trade union organization and legislation represented political
means of dealing with the problems of women workers. Their weak position in the labor market stemmed from the lack of training that
limited them to unskilled work, where under the threat of replacement
by cheaper labor or by machines, they were at the mercy of the employer. While women workers saw the choice as between low wages and
no wages, philanthropists such as Helen Bosanquet and the members of
the Women's Industrial Council in England, and rich Americans such as
Grace Dodge strongly urged technical training that would convert
women from unskilled to skilled workers. Equipped with marketable
skills, they would compete in the job market instead of being its
victims.

Efforts to diversify women's work by encouraging young girls to
consider a wide variety of possible occupations accompanied the campaign for technical training. Dictionaries that listed and described
jobs women had entered or might enter ranged from extremely practical
guides, such as that provided for Charity Organization Society workers
(entry 246) suggesting bookbinding and jam manufacture, to wide-
ranging compilations like the Women's Institute publication (entry

237), which cheerfully described occupations ranging from the "caller" who walked the streets in the morning waking poor people who had no clocks, to the doctor. Grace Hoadley Dodge's dictionary (entry 381) suggested a fanciful variety that included dairy farming and portrait painting, among other professions.

Social investigators strove to dispel the myth that women worked only for secondary income and therefore did not require a living wage; they demonstrated statistically, over and over again, that many women were indeed breadwinners for themselves and others. Nevertheless, all of these efforts were hampered by the fact that many women themselves thought of their occupations as temporary--to last until they married or to tide the family over a financial crisis.

Clara E. Collet drew attention to the plight of middle-class working women in England. Invisible to many, frequently ill-equipped for employment by their education and upbringing, these "redundant" women found financial independence hard to achieve. The kind of work they did (teaching, working in shops, or office clerical work) required a certain standard of dress, their social class demanded a respectable address, and often they stayed within their budget only by inadequate diet and no holidays. Alice Zimmern (entry 318) described some interesting experiments to provide suitable living accommodations and relief from housekeeping duties, but Collet and others warned that subsidizing such accommodations would merely perpetuate low salaries. Charlotte Perkins Gilman in writings and lectures proposed new kinds of living and working arrangements that would reduce or eliminate traditional housekeeping. Her ideas were received eagerly in England as well as in the United States, and some experiments with kitchenless houses and cooperative housekeeping schemes occurred. Novelists like Emma Brooke and Sabine Baring-Gould wrote about these women and their problems, while Grant Allen (a pseudonym) created a dashing heroine who started from Girton College with twopence, and through audacity and ingenuity achieved an unconventional career (entry 4).

The differences and similarities in women's work and its effects and ramifications in Britain and the United States have been inadequately studied. By presenting side-by-side sources for both countries, I hope to facilitate and encourage such comparative work. The influence of the feminist movement on the work women did and on the demands made by working women has only begun to be explored. The Women's Trade Union Leagues in the two countries were closely related in their early development, but other organizations that provided the setting for interaction between women of different social classes should also be examined comparatively. Factors of class, race, and ethnicity differ in importance in Britain and in the United States, and here, too, comparisons might yield interesting results. Attitudes toward the family and child-raising and of employers toward women are other areas in which comparison would be enlightening.

Introduction

My survey of printed sources has revealed much interesting primary material for the study of the history of women's work from 1890 to 1914. The historical works mentioned here and in the bibliography illustrate the possibilities for illuminating previously unexplored aspects of the subject through careful and imaginative use of such material.

Over and over, similarities appear between the problems and concerns of working women at the turn of the century and those that women face today. "These voices are beginning only now to emerge from silence into half articulate speech," wrote Virginia Woolf in her introduction to Life As We Have Known It, a collection of reminiscences by English working women. "These lives are still half hidden in profound obscurity."* The spotlight that has rested on a few major figures needs to broaden its focus to illuminate that obscurity.

---

*Virginia Woolf, "Introductory Letter to Margaret Llewelyn Davies," Life As We Have Known It, ed. Margaret Llewelyn Davies (New York: W. W. Norton, 1975), p. xxxix.

Women's Work in Great Britain

1   ABBOTT, EDITH. "Municipal Employment of Unemployed Women in
    London." Journal of Political Economy 15 (1907):513-30.
        An experimental program was set up in London intended to
    provide employment for women temporarily out of work by
    establishing workrooms. Abbott analyses the applicants and
    participants and finds that in fact they were mostly older,
    unskilled, and widowed. She argues that to give a positive
    impact, the workrooms should include only younger women and
    should train them in new skills to make them employable.

2   ABERDEEN, ISHBEL. "Household Clubs: an Experiment."
    Nineteenth Century 31 (1892):391-98.
        The lack of social life was a frequent complaint of ser-
    vants, especially in country houses. Lady Aberdeen describes
    one solution, a club organized for the servants of a large
    household. Planned activities included singing, learning
    skills such as drawing and woodworking, lectures by members
    of the group or by the master's houseguests, and social
    events. There is no indication of how long the club lasted
    or whether it was imitated in other households.

3   ADLER, N., and TAWNEY, R. H. Boy and Girl Labour. London:
    Women's Industrial Council, 1909. 17 pp.
        This pamphlet criticizes the employment of young boys
    and girls in unskilled work and recommends required train-
    ing for girls in skilled trades, "domestic economy," Eng-
    lish, drawing, and physical exercise.

4   ALLEN, CHARLES GRANT BLAIRFINDIE [Grant Allen]. Miss Cayley's
    Adventures. London: New York: Grant Richards, 1899.
    330 pp.
        A woman university graduate who sets out with twopence
    to travel and seek her fortune is the heroine of this light
    and funny novel. She travels as an old lady's companion,
    sells bicycles in Switzerland on commission from an enter-
    prising American businessman, and performs daring rescues.
    The book parallels and gently satirizes the standard novel
    of a young man's adventures.

5   ANDERSON, ADELAIDE MARY. <u>Women in the Factory, an Administra-
    tive Adventure, 1893 to 1921</u>. London: John Murray, 1922.
    316 pp.
        Anderson, one of the first women factory inspectors,
    writes about her work. Women were appointed as factory
    inspectors in the belief that women workers would find it
    easier to report violations of the Factory Acts to other
    women than to men. Anderson describes the conditions she
    saw and the way she worked. Tact and personal influence,
    she claims, sometimes persuaded managers to improve working
    conditions more successfully than law enforcement. Middle-
    of-the-night raids to catch employers in the act of violat-
    ing the law contributed to her sense of adventure on the
    job.

6   APPRENTICESHIP AND SKILLED EMPLOYMENT ASSOCIATION. <u>Trades for
    London Girls and How to Enter Them</u>. London: Longmans
    Green, 1914. 167 pp.
        This compilation was intended to assist parents in
    choosing occupations for their daughters. For each job it
    realistically describes conditions of work, apprenticeship
    or training opportunities, physical requirements, wages,
    and neighborhoods in which the trade is concentrated.
    Teaching, clerical work, and shop work are included, as
    well as industrial work.

7   ATKINSON, MABEL. <u>The Economic Foundations of the Women's
    Movement</u>. Fabian Tracts, no. 175. London: Fabian Society,
    1914. 24 pp.
        The decline of the family as a work unit, a result of
    changes in the system of industry, has caused two problems
    for women: middle-class women have been excluded from jobs,
    and working-class women have been exploited by industry.
    Atkinson proposes that socialism and feminism together can
    provide solutions to both problems, and endorses government
    support of childbearing women. Bibliography.

8   BARING-GOULD, SABINE. <u>The Frobishers</u>. London: Methuen,
    1901. 308 pp.
        A novel of the potteries in North Staffordshire argues
    for the good influence of educated upper-class people upon
    working-class people.

9   BARLOW, MAY S. "Report of an Enquiry into the Supply of and
    Demand for Nurses for Little Children." <u>Women's Industrial
    News</u> 55 (1911):95-104.
        Reporting on the results of a survey of registry offices,
    Barlow concludes with a recommendation that schools be es-
    tablished to train young women as children's nurses.

10 BATESON, MARGARET. <u>Professional Women upon their Professions</u>.
    London: Horace Cox, 1895. 133 pp.
        These short interviews with women in various professions
    originally appeared in a journal and were intended to give
    young girls an idea of the variety of possible occupations.
    The most interesting are with women in less common profes-
    sions: the only woman stockbroker in London, a portrait
    photographer, an accountant, a lady who not only manages
    a laundry but trains other ladies in that occupation.
    Twenty-six women were interviewed.

11 BELL, FLORENCE [Lady Bell]. <u>At the Works, a Study of a Manu-</u>
    <u>facturing Town</u>. London: E. Arnold, 1907. Reprint. New
    York: Augustus M. Kelley, 1969. 272 pp.
        A sympathetic observer describes the lives of Middles-
    brough iron-mill workers and their families. There was no
    work for women in the mills, and nearly all of them married
    early as there was a surplus of men; some were employed,
    mostly at sewing trades. Their household duties and their
    health are described in some detail. There is a chapter on
    what people read, and one on gambling, which was common
    among women. This is a far more optimistic picture than
    the earlier American one presented in Rebecca Harding
    Davis's <u>Life in the Iron Mills</u>. (See also Jim Leonard,
    "Lady Bell and Edwardian Middlesbrough," entry 169.)

12 BERKMAN, JOYCE AVRECH. <u>Olive Schreiner: Feminism on the</u>
    <u>Frontier</u>. St. Alban's, Vt.: Eden Press Women's Publica-
    tions, 1979. 88 pp. Bibliography.
        Schreiner denied gender differentiation except as so-
    cially imposed. She saw women's parasitism as not only
    limiting to women but dangerous to offspring through trans-
    mission of passive traits. Her view of women's roles fails,
    on the whole, to take working-class women's position into
    account. She believed that the actions of individual women
    would have a cumulative effect in bringing about reform.
    As a pacifist, she could not support the militant suffra-
    gettes, yet she understood the justification of their
    actions. Her ambivalence isolated her from other feminists
    in her own time, although present-day readers find her to
    have been exceptionally prescient. Bibliography.

13 BESANT, WALTER. <u>Children of Gibeon</u>. 2d ed. 3 vols. London:
    Chatto & Windus, 1886.
        Widely read in its day, this novel concerns a working-
    class girl and the daughter of a lady who were brought up
    together; only the lady knows which is which. One of the
    girls goes to live with her supposed sister, a home-working
    seamstress. Besant takes the opportunity to describe exten-
    sively the life of the poor, the conditions of home-work,
    and the exploitation of the workers, and to present possible
    means of improvement.

14 BILLINGTON GREIG, TERESA. The Militant Suffrage Movement.
    London: Frank Palmer, 1911, 219 pp.
        An exmilitant criticizes the Pankhursts' authoritarianism
    and techniques, objecting to the casting out of working
    women by the Women's Social and Political Union.

15 BIRD, M. MOSTYN. Woman at Work: a Study of the Different
    Ways of Earning a Living Open to Women. London: Chapman &
    Hall, 1911. 257 pp.
        Intended to encourage girls to think about work as a
    permanent part of their lives and choose responsibly, this
    book describes a variety of careers in the fields of manu-
    facture, distribution, service, the professions, the arts,
    and philanthropy. Many of the sections are brief, but the
    variety of suggestions is interesting. "Independent occupa-
    tions" such as gardening, tea-room and shop management,
    and interior decorating are included. Philanthropic work
    as a paid profession is a growing field. Librarianship is
    described as a difficult field for women to enter.

16 No entry.

17 BLACK, CLEMENTINA. "The Coming Factory Act." Contemporary
    Review 59 (1891):710-17.
        The author compares the proposed British Factory Act
    with similar legislation in New York State.

18 _____. "London's Tailoresses." Economic Journal 14 (1904):
    555-67.
        This report of a 1903 Women's Industrial Council inquiry
    describes conditions of work for women in the tailoring
    trade in various parts of London--West End, East End,
    Whitechapel, and Soho--in workshops and in home-work.
    Small workshops and home-work, which escaped legal regula-
    tion, had the worst working conditions. Women waistcoat-
    makers had the best conditions, in the reporter's opinion.

19 _____. Married Women's Work, being the Report of an Enquiry
    Undertaken by the Women's Industrial Council (Incorporated).
    London: G. Bell & Sons, 1915. 292 pp.
        Based on a 1909-10 investigation in ten industrial cities
    as well as rural districts, the report concludes that mar-
    ried women should not be discouraged from working and should
    be paid enough to live decently and avoid constant worry.
    The investigators found that healthy, intelligent women who
    work outside the home generally enjoy it and are the best
    household managers. A great variety of occupations were
    studied (makers of tennis ball covers, for example); infor-
    mation about wages and living conditions is amplified by
    frequent personal observation.

20 _____. "The National Insurance Bill." Women's Industrial
News, n.s. 55 (October 1911):135-36.
In a brief, strongly worded critique, Black argues that
insurance coverage for women in the bill under consideration is so inadequate that women might better be left out
of it altogether.

21 _____. Sweated Industry and the Minimum Wage. London:
Duckworth, 1907. 281 pp.
Emigration, consumers' leagues, cooperation, and thrift
cannot solve the problems of underpaid workers. Employers
waste resources (the workers) by demanding too much and pay-
ing too little. The cotton industry demonstrates that English manufacturers can pay a living wage for reasonable
hours of work and still maintain the lead in a world industry. When poor, overworked people need help, they draw
on the strength and resources of other poor people. The
author disagrees with Helen Bosanquet's theory that the
poor only need to be taught efficiency to improve their
living conditions.

22 BLACKBURN, HELEN. Women's Suffrage, a Record of the Women's
Suffrage Movement in the British Isles, with Biographical
Sketches of Miss Becker. London: Williams & Norgate,
1902. 298 pp.
Relating the history of women's political position in
Britain from early times to 1900, this book gives a particularly clear account of the frustration of the years
1890-1900, as Parliament avoided discussing the question
of women's suffrage year after year. It is a good source
of information on the committees and people involved. The
bibliography cites many pamphlets and other ephemera.

23 BLEASE, WALTER LYON. The Emancipation of English Women.
London: Constable, 1910. 281 pp.
The author reviews the history of women's position in
England since the Restoration and concludes that the apparent inferiority of women to men is the result of unequal
education and upbringing. The violent action of militant
suffragettes is defended as a reaction to the failure of
government to take women's demands seriously.

24 BLYTHELL, DUNCAN. The Sweated Trades: Outwork in Nineteenth-
Century Britain. New York: St. Martin's Press, 1978.
287 pp.
Blythell's thorough description and analysis of outwork
and the economic and political situation that permitted it
offers much detail and allows no romantic view of this op-
pressive system.

25 BONDFIELD, MARGARET G. "Conditions under which Shop Assistants
    Work." Economic Journal 9 (1899):277-86.
        Under the living-in system that prevailed in many city
    shops, shop assistants (clerks) were required to stay in
    dormitorylike accommodations provided by the management.
    Lack of privacy, inadequate food, and the restrictions im-
    posed by house rules were frequent complaints. The shop
    assistant who was fired lost a place to live as well.
    Bondfield provides considerable detail on good as well as
    bad establishments.

26 _____. A Life's Work. London: Hutchinson, 1951. 368 pp.
        Margaret G. Bondfield was a leader of the women's trade
    union movement, assistant secretary of the Shop Assistant's
    Union, and active in the International Labour Party. In
    later years she was a strong pacifist and (after World War
    I) the first woman Labour Member of Parliament. This auto-
    biography includes personal recollections of many people
    with whom she worked in the Women's Trade Union League and
    other organizations. Her impressions of the United States
    are recorded in two chapters about a 1910 speaking tour of
    Boston; Lawrence, Massachusetts (a center of the labor move-
    ment); Atlanta; and Chicago, where she went to Hull House.

27 _____. Shop Workers and the Vote. London: The People's
    Suffrage Federation, 1911. 18 pp.
        Shop assistants were deprived of the right to vote be-
    cause living-in arrangements did not satisfy the residency
    requirement and they were likely to have to move often. As
    a large class of workers, Bondfield argues that they repre-
    sent a strong argument for suffrage for both sexes.

28 _____. "What Shop Workers Want from Parliament." Women's
    Trade Union Review, no. 70 (July 1908):12-17.
        Shop assistants need legislation to limit hours of work;
    to require compensation in money, not in goods or living
    accommodations; to bar restrictions on subsequent employ-
    ment; and to regulate employers' references.

29 BOSANQUET, HELEN. "The Economics of Women's Work and Wages."
    National Liberal Club, Political and Economic Circle.
    Transactions, vol. 5, part 14. London: P. S. King, 1907.
    16 pp.
        To improve the position of women in the labor market,
    Bosanquet proposes raising the lowest wages and reorganiz-
    ing factory work, using machine technology to make the
    lowest level of work more challenging and less degrading.
    She points out that many women work for necessary income,
    not pocket money, and that women's work as housewives and
    mothers deserves more respect than it now receives.

30 _____. Rich and Poor. London: Macmillan, 1896. 216 pp.
By describing the life of one London parish, Bosanquet
intends to "present a concrete idea of the conditions under
which social work must be carried on." Problems of women
include management of the family income, home-work, concerns of working mothers, and the need for training to do
skilled work.

31 _____. "Report of the Special Committee on the Industrial
Employment of Women." Charity Organization Review 8
(December 1900):407-8.
Bosanquet complains that other agencies failed to
cooperate with the Charity Organization Society's investigation; the Women's Industrial Council, the Central
Bureau for the Employment of Women, and the National Society for Promoting the Employment of Women were not interested in pooling information.

32 _____. The Standard of Life, and Other Reprinted Essays.
2d ed. London: Macmillan, 1906. 371 pp.
In two essays in this collection, "The Education of
Women" (pp. 280-302) and "Industrial Training of Women"
(pp. 303-20), the author urges technical and academic education for women. She argues that (1) such training will
prevent them from marrying solely for economic security or
from being limited to unskilled jobs in which they are competing with or being replaced by machines, and (2) increased
employment of women improves the economy by providing them
with more money to spend.

33 _____. "A Study in Women's Wages." Economic Journal 12
(March 1902):42-49.
The low wages paid to women result in the necessity for
public support, especially in those "irregular" trades that
have a slack season. Bosanquet believes recipients of public support are more neglectful of their homes than "independent" women. She also criticizes charities that supply
the poor with clothes made by gentlewomen because they
usurp a source of earnings for poor women. This is a good
example of Bosanquet's Charity Organization Society
philosophy.

34 _____. "Wages and Housekeeping." In Methods of Social
Advance, edited by C. S. Loch, pp. 131-46. London:
Macmillan, 1904.
Focusing on the woman as household manager, Bosanquet
endorses the cooperative store as encouraging saving of
money and preventing poor families from getting into debt
through credit buying.

35   BOUCHERETT, E. JESSIE. "Lead Poisoning in Pottery Work."
      Englishwomen's Review 30 (15 April 1899):98-102.
          Boucherett opposes legislation that prevents women from
      being employed in trades in which lead is used. She points
      out that in other countries the hazards of working with
      lead are controlled by improving conditions in the work-
      place rather than by putting people out of work.

36   BOUCHERETT, E. JESSIE, and BLACKBURN, HELEN, eds. The Condi-
      tion of Working Women and the Factory Acts. London:
      Elliot Stock, 1896. 84 pp.
          The Factory Acts discriminate against women, especially
      laundresses, tailoresses, and those in the mineral water
      bottling trade where inability to work overtime means loss
      of the job. Keeping women out of industries in which lead
      is used is unfair, as no other employment is available to
      them. This is an example of a point of view thoroughly
      opposed to protective legislation.

37   "Bow and Spear: Women's Lodging Houses and the Woman Worker."
      Englishwoman 8 (1910):139.
          Advocating regulation of common lodging houses in which
      women workers lived, the writer proposes a system of inspec-
      tion and a requirement that male lodging-house keepers must
      be married.

38   BRADBY, L. BARBARA, and BLACK, ANNE. "Women Compositors and
      the Factory Acts." Economic Journal 9 (1899):260-66.
          The authors find that the Factory Acts restriction on
      hours women are permitted to work has not adversely affected
      their employment as compositors; employers do not hire women
      in this industry based on the lack of physical strength or
      training and because marriage is likely to end their careers.

39   BRITISH ASSOCIATION FOR LABOUR LEGISLATION. Report on the
      Administration of Labour Laws in the United Kingdom.
      London: Twentieth Century Press, 1908. 47 pp.
          Written as a response to an International Association
      for Labour Legislation questionnaire, this report summa-
      rizes the application of labor laws, the work of the in-
      spectors, general administration, cooperation from factory
      workers, and proposed reforms. Although the text supplies
      no new information, there are many tables giving statistics
      on numbers of inspectors for various geographical areas and
      trades, visits paid, prosecutions, and penalties.

40   BROOKE, EMMA. Transition. London: William Heinemann, 1895.
      330 pp.
          This is a novel about a Girton graduate with lofty
      scholarly ambitions who goes to work as a schoolteacher
      because of financial need. She emerges from her snobbery

under the influence of a fellow teacher and becomes interested in socialism (while her friend becomes involved with
anarchists). The life of schoolmistresses is well described.
The friendship of the two women is interesting, and so is
the view of radical politics. Although the story is sometimes melodramatic, the author has a sense of humor.

41   BULLEY, AGNES AMY, and WHITBY, MARGARET. Women's Work.
     Preface by Lady Dilke. London: Methuen & Co., 1894.
     172 pp.
         This short discussion of women's work describes pleasant
     and unpleasant aspects, earnings, and prospects in a wide
     range of occupations. The authors have a bias in favor of
     trade unions and endorse protective legislation. Where
     possible, they prefer to see the married woman "queen of
     her own hearth." A Directory of Women's Trade Unions, with
     the number of members of each, if known, is appended.

42   BURDETT-COUTTS, ANGELA G., ed. Woman's Mission. New York:
     Scribner, 1893. 485 pp.
         This report was prepared for the Chicago Exhibition of
     1893; the essays by various authors encompass all forms of
     volunteer work done by women in Great Britain. Although
     they tend to the sentimental and self-congratulatory, the
     variety of activity is impressive, and the essays reveal
     as much about the philanthropists as about those they
     served. A few interesting examples: women who established
     knitting and sewing industries in Ireland to teach a skill
     and provide employment for destitute Irish women; the Royal
     School of Art Needlework, which trained gentlewomen who
     needed a means of earning a livelihood; and the Metropoli-
     tan Association for Befriending Young Servants, under the
     auspices of which 1,100 lady visitors kept watchful eyes on
     the moral welfare of servant girls. An appendix lists phil-
     anthropic organizations and identifies them by the category
     of people they served.

43   BURNETT, JOHN, ed. Useful Toil: Autobiographies of Working
     People from the 1820s to the 1920s. London: Allen Lane,
     1974. 364 pp.
         Many of the autobiographies collected here are of the
     period after 1914. The introductory essay on domestic ser-
     vants provides a good analysis of the duties and wages of
     servants, the structure of households, and the reasons for
     declining desirability of this occupation in the late
     nineteenth century.

44   BUTLER, CHRISTINA VIOLET. Domestic Service: an Enquiry by
     the Women's Industrial Council. Report by C. V. Butler,
     with a supplementary chapter by Lady Marie Willoughby
     de Broke. London: G. Bell & Sons, 1916. 148 pp.

9

This survey conducted in 1914 investigated opinions of servants and their employers about aspects of domestic service: the personal side, liberty, companionship, interest, and status; wages and other compensation; and employment registries, references, and terms of work. The data, which reveal a range of opinions with many direct quotes, came from responses by 708 employers and 566 servants, as well as "hundreds" of additional letters. Among the points emphasized are the importance of the mistress's administrative skill and concern for servants' welfare; the power of upper servants in a large household over lower servants; the difficulty of regulating this occupation. Hotel keepers as well as private employers were included; the questionnaires are appended.

45   CADBURY, EDWARD; MATHESON, M. CECILE; and SHANN, GEORGE. Women's Work and Wages: a Phase of Life in an Industrial City. London: T. Fisher Unwin, 1906. 368 pp.
    Women workers in Birmingham, both in factories and at home, were the subject of this survey. Information was collected on a large variety of occupations (excluding textiles, not an important industry in Birmingham), their hours, wages, conditions of work, and status of the occupation in the eyes of the workers. The metal trades receive special attention. A combination of statistics with interviews and observations creates a useful total picture, and concludes that denying minimum wages will lead to higher prices for goods.
    Appendixes include a table of trades and weekly wages; tables relating to age of marriage; and a table of weights and measurements of girls who have had athletic training. It was hoped that the study would provide a standard of comparison for the future, in addition to suggesting reforms.

46   CALLEN, ANTHEA. Women Artists of the Arts and Crafts Movement 1870-1914. New York: Pantheon Books, 1979. 232 pp. Published in Great Britain as Angel in the Studio: Women in the Arts and Crafts Movement 1870-1914. London: The Architectural Press, 1979.
    This careful study is the first to concentrate on the role of women in the Arts and Crafts Movement. After a discussion of working-class women, gentlewomen, and lady philanthropists and a survey of design education, Callen devotes a chapter to each of the crafts of ceramics, needlework, lacemaking, jewelry, woodworking and interior design, and the book crafts. Many illustrations. Bibliography. Biographical notes.

47   CARPENTER, EDWARD. Woman and Her Place in a Free Society. Manchester: Labour Press Society, 1894. 41 pp.

Carpenter believes that women's "nature" is different
from men's. He wants women to be free from domestic slavery and urges them to seek experience of the world as well
as education. Increased sexual freedom will discourage
prostitution; women who have more freedom will be better
mothers.

48 CATRIONA [pseud.]. "How I Began to Earn My Living." Labour
Woman, no. 2 (June 1913):22-3.
Beginning at the age of eighteen as a bookkeeper in a
dressmaking establishment in a small country town, the
author moved on to dressmaking in Glasgow.

49 CHAPMAN, SYDNEY J. The Lancashire Cotton Industry, a Study in
Economic Development. Economic Series, no. 1. Manchester:
Manchester University Press, 1904. 309 pp.
This history traces the growth of the cotton industry
including production, marketing, and distribution of income.
It contains little information about women (Chapman seems
to assume that they should be kept out of skilled jobs and
trade union membership) but is helpful for information on
the industry as a whole. Bibliography.

50 COLLET, CLARA ELIZABETH. The Economic Position of Educated
Working Women. South Place Ethical Society Publications
no. 25, pp. 205-16. London: E. W. Allen, 1890.
Collet, the social investigator, freely expresses her
own point of view in this discourse delivered in South
Place Chapel, Finsbury, E. C. Educated women should be
encouraged to enter a greater variety of fields (business
or farming, for example) and should be able to earn enough
to live on so that they will not be tempted to marry for a
livelihood. Intelligent women are not necessarily the best
wives; they should have time to find their own work and
maturity. Women benefit from the honest criticism that
goes with paid work; volunteers are not always told the
truth about the quality of their work.

51 _____. Educated Working Women: Essays on the Economic Position of Women Workers in the Middle Classes. London:
P. S. King, 1902. 143 pp.
These essays originally appeared in journals between
1890 and 1900. "The Economic Position of Educated Working
Women" and "The Expenditure of Middle Class Working Women"
argue that women must be paid enough for financial independence and that their parents should not be expected to
subsidize their work. This means enough money for proper
clothes and food, and holidays to restore energy. Not all
educated women should be teachers. "Prospects of Marriage
for Women" (1892) supports her insistence on financial independence with statistics showing that more middle-class

women than working-class women will remain unmarried.
Other essays advocate selection of occupations for married
women that will permit some years' absence for child-
rearing, and making use of the experience of older women.

52 · _____. "Women's Work in Leeds." Economic Journal 1 (1891):
460-73.
Women in Leeds worked in cloth and clothing manufacture,
and rag-sorting. Collet compares earnings with those of
East London women, and gives information on backgrounds
(fathers' and mothers' occupations and origins).

53 "Conference on the National Insurance Bill." National Union
of Women Workers. Occasional Paper, no. 55 (July 1911):
13-28.
Provisions for maternity and care of married women and
widows are criticized. The method of coverage through
approved societies leaves out many women whose only alternative is limited coverage as "deposit contributors."

54 CONGRÈS INTERNATIONAL DES OEUVRES ET INSTITUTIONS FÉMININES.
2d, Paris, du 19 au 23 juin 1900. Compte Rendu des Travaux.
4 vols. Paris: Imprimerie Typographique Charles Blot,
1902.
The conference had five sections: (1) Philanthropie et
Economie Sociale; (2) Legislation et Morale; (3) Education
Individuelle, Education Sociale, Pedagogie; (4) Travail;
(5) Arts, Lettres, Sciences. The fourth section included
discussion of freedom to work, salary, ways to encourage
women's work at home, cooperative societies, and the value
of agricultural training for women. In the fifth section,
papers were presented on women in the arts and literature,
women librarians and curators, the current situation of
women in the sciences, and means of teaching family and
child hygiene. Among the speakers were Jane Addams, Helen
Bosanquet, and Margaret Macdonald. A question on municipal
baths and women's dress reform created a diversion in the
midst of the discussion on women in science. The
Bibliothèque Marguerite Duran, Paris, has correspondence
and press clippings relating to the Congrès as well as
the published proceedings.

55 CONWAY, JILL. "Stereotypes of Femininity in a Theory of
Sexual Evolution." Victorian Studies 14 (1970):47-62.
Patrick Geddes's theory of men's and women's social
roles assumed male rationality and female intuition; male
tendency to dissipate energy and female tendency to con-
serve it. He predicted an evolution toward a "utopia of
the emotions." He feared that by forcing women into men's
roles, industrialization might spoil female instincts.
Women's work should be altruism; to channel their resources

into society, Geddes advocated temperance in intercourse as
a method of limiting children. Jane Addams was an important follower of Geddes. In England, Hobhouse moved away
from Geddes's positivism toward a more conservative view,
accepting the idea that the procreative function arrested
female development.

56   COOK, CHRIS. <u>Sources in British Political History 1900-1951</u>.
     4 vols. London: Macmillan, 1975.
        The first volume of this guide lists the archives of
     organizations and societies; remaining volumes locate per-
     sonal papers of political figures.

57   CRAWFORD, EMILY. "Journalism as a Profession for Women."
     <u>Contemporary Review</u> 64 (1893):362-71.
        This realistic assessment of the physical and mental
     requirements of journalism concludes by urging women to
     enter the profession. (Also cited as entry 374.)

58   CREIGHTON, LOUISE. <u>The Social Disease and How to Fight It</u>.
     London: Longmans Green, 1914. 87 pp.
        Creighton appeals for higher wages for working girls to
     prevent their becoming prostitutes, community education
     about venereal disease, and improved medical treatment for
     venereal disease.

59   _____. <u>Women's Work for the Church and for the State</u>. Pan-
     Anglican papers, no. 7, London: Society for Promoting
     Christian Knowledge, 1907. 12 pp.
        Issues under consideration for the 1908 Pan-Anglican
     Congress included the need for the Anglican church to
     appeal to the highly educated independent woman by offer-
     ing work that uses her skills in parochial tasks, foreign
     missions, and religious teaching, both volunteer and paid.
     Training should be offered. The author disapproves of mar-
     ried women's employment except in cases of extreme need,
     but thinks busy, trained women make better wives and
     mothers.

60   CROSSICK, GEOFFREY, ed. <u>The Lower Middle Class in England,
     1870-1914</u>. London: Croom Helm, 1976. 213 pp.
        This collection of essays with a sociological perspec-
     tive offers some interesting analyses of lower middle-class
     behavior. These were people whose employment was service
     to the middle and upper classes (shops, offices, etc.); to
     succeed they had to dress and behave like the people they
     served. Outside of work, they maintained that image by
     retreating from public places to the privacy of the home;
     they kept up appearances and "keep themselves to themselves."
        Crossick's own essay claims that it is impossible to
     locate the female white-collar worker in his analysis of

stratification, since the family is the unit of analysis
and the man's occupation is the main indicator of family
status. "More information about the marital status, social
origins and family structure of female employees would help
an understanding of the effect of female workers upon the
perceived status structure."

61 CUNNINGHAM, GAIL. The New Woman and the Victorian Novel.
    New York: Harper & Row; London: The Macmillan Press,
    1978. 172 pp.
       A study of the changing image of woman in the novel,
    this book examines the work of such writers of the nine-
    teenth and early twentieth centuries as Grant Allen, Emma
    Brooke, George Egerton, George Gissing, Thomas Hardy, and
    H. G. Wells, with attention to their often ambivalent atti-
    tudes about sexuality, marriage, and the independence of
    women. Bibliography.

62 CUTHBERT, NORMAN H. The Lace Makers Society: a Study of Trade
    Unionism in the British Lace Industry, 1760-1960.
    Nottingham: Amalgamated Society of Operative Lace Makers
    and Auxiliary Workers, 1960. 293 pp.
       A thorough history of trade unions in the lacemaking
    industry. Part 1 covers the period 1760-1914. The women's
    union was a separate organization during this period.
    Women were (and still are) restricted to certain jobs in
    lacemaking. Although there is no bibliography, abundant
    footnotes are helpful guides to sources. Further work on
    women in this industry would be helpful.

63 DANGERFIELD, GEORGE. The Strange Death of Liberal England.
    London: Constable, 1935. Reprint. London: MacGibbon &
    Kee, 1966. 420 pp.
       This essential book on England from 1906 to 1914 empha-
    sizes the issues of suffrage, Irish home rule, and trade
    unions. All, Dangerfield argues, represent a casting away
    of respectability. The Liberals kept trying to compromise
    and so destroyed themselves. Particular attention is given
    to Sylvia Pankhurst and the working women she encouraged to
    join the movement; they nearly succeeded in gaining the
    suffrage in 1914, but the war intervened. Bibliography.

64 DAVIDOFF, LEONORE. The Best Circles: Society, Etiquette and
    the Season. London: Croom Helm, 1973. 127 pp.
       In the later chapters of this lively sociological account
    of English society Davidoff examines the difficulties of
    upper-class women who needed or wanted to work. They lacked
    not only minimal skill and opportunities, but also any ex-
    perience of working among groups of people, since most of
    them had been taught by governesses and thus denied even
    classroom experience. Bibliography.

65   _____. "Mastered for Life: Servant and Wife in Victorian
      and Edwardian England." Journal of Social History 7
      (1974):406-28.
          Both servants and wives were in a subordinate position
      to someone who exerted total control. Many women moved
      from paternal control to that of a master or mistress and
      then to a husband's, never experiencing life otherwise.
      They received total support in exchange for total subordi-
      nation. Servants and married women were among the last
      groups to be allowed full participation in civil society.
      Davidoff draws interesting parallels, concentrating her
      study especially on servant girls who married.

66   DAVIDOFF, LEONORE, and HAWTHORN, RUTH. A Day in the Life of a
      Victorian Domestic Servant. London: George Allen & Unwin,
      1976. 94 pp.
          An imaginary "tweeny" (a young girl whose work was to
      assist the cook and the housemaid) goes through a day's
      work. An incident about a missing pendant adds drama and
      demonstrates the lack of trust between mistress and ser-
      vant. Intended for young readers, this is a good, detailed
      account of the young servant's life.

67   DAVIES, C. STELLA. North Country Bred: a Working-Class
      Family Chronicle. London: Routledge & Kegan Paul, 1963.
      256 pp.
          Davies's training as an economic historian enhances this
      autobiography. A member of a politically radical family,
      active in the Co-operative Movement, she grew up in
      Manchester and worked there as a telephone operator be-
      fore the First World War. Family members cooperated in
      patching together ways to earn money and care for the
      children.

68   DAVIES, MARGARET LLEWELLYN, ed. Life As We Have Known It, by
      Co-operative Working Women. With an Introductory Letter by
      Virginia Woolf. London: Leonard and Virginia Woolf, 1931.
      Reprint. New York: W. W. Norton, 1975. 141 pp.
          Women members of the Co-operative Guild reminisce about
      their lives and their work in interesting firsthand
      accounts.

69   _____. Maternity: Letters from Working Women. London:
      G. Bell & Sons, 1915. Reprint. London: Virago, 1978.
      212 pp.
          Women of the Co-operative Guild describe their experi-
      ences in childbirth and child rearing.

70   DAVIES, MARGARET LLEWELLYN. Why Working Women Need the Vote.
      Paper read at the Southern Sectional Conference, London,
      15 March 1897. Manchester: Women's Co-operative Guild,
      1897.

Women need the vote in order to bring about reform in
social and labor legislation, and to enable them to act as
free, independent human beings.

71 DAVIN, ANNA. "Imperialism and Motherhood." History Workshop
Journal 5 (1978):9-65.
A concern for the need of the nation for a healthy and
increasing population in the early twentieth century led
to emphasis on the importance of motherhood. The state's
interest in raising clean, healthy children manifested itself in home inspection, education of mothers, and opposition to mothers' employment. "Surrogate mother" occupations
such as teaching and nursing were urged on women who did not
have children of their own. Davin cites this example to
demonstrate the use of ideology to discourage or encourage
married women's work outside the home, according to the
needs of the labor market.

72 DEVERELL, EDITH M. "Slate Clubs." Economic Journal 9 (1899):
266-77.
Slate clubs were small, simple organizations into which
working people paid a regular sum toward some specific
benefit: burial or convalescent home insurance, or the
purchase of particular goods such as clothes. Meetings
were held weekly, often in a pub; members joined for the
social life as well as the benefits, and might join several
clubs. Deverell criticizes the ineptness, poor organization, and even fraud that often characterized such groups,
and argues that the larger friendly societies or trade
unions filled the insurance function more efficiently.
The reader can glimpse the attraction of the slate club
as a means of managing very small budgets and as a social
outlet.

73 DILKE, EMILIA F. S. The Industrial Position of Women.
London: Women's Trade Union League, n.d. 15 pp.
This pamphlet, of interest chiefly as a document of
Dilke's activity, cites abuses of women in a variety of
trades as an argument for organization and training of
women workers.

74 _____. Trades Unions for Women. London: Women's Trade
Union League, n.d. 12 pp.
Dilke discusses the work of the Women's Trade Union
League, problems of organizing women, and her opposition
to mothers working unless it is essential. She endorses
inclusion of women in male unions whenever possible.

75 DIX, GERTRUDE. The Image Breakers. London: Heinemann, 1900.
284 pp.

Two women radicals deal with political action, work, and love in this rather overcharged novel. The male characters are quite stereotyped, but the women's struggles to maintain integrity and pursue their work without being submerged in a man's life are interesting. Leslie Ardent, an artist, finally arrives at an equal relationship with Redgold; Rosemary, the other woman, comes to a grim end, separated from her cause-obsessed lover, and guardian to a paranoid boy anarchist. Lots of storms, dark, wind, fire, or sunshine, as appropriate.

76 DOLLÉANS, EDOUARD, and CROZIER, MICHEL. <u>Mouvements Ouvrier et Socialiste. Chronologie et Bibliographie: Angleterre, France, Allemagne, États-Unis, 1750-1918</u>. Paris: Les Editions Ouvrières, 1950. 381 pp.
    The scope of this chronology and bibliography of workers' movements includes England and the United States. Chapters 8 and 9 deal with America between 1860 and 1918, and chapter 12 with England between 1899 and 1914. There are useful citations to documents (proceedings of congresses, etc.) and journals, as well as histories and statements of position. Name index.

77 DONNISON, JEAN. <u>Midwives and Medical Men: a History of Interprofessional Rivalries and Women's Rights</u>. London: Heinemann, 1977. 250 pp.
    From the 1880s until 1902 when the Midwives Act was passed, English physicians battled for legislation governing licensing and regulation of midwives. Donnison presents a convincing argument that the physicians were prompted largely by a desire to eliminate midwives from competition for patients. They succeeded to a large extent, although in recent years there has been a revival of the midwives' profession.

78 DRAKE, BARBARA. <u>Women in Trade Unions</u>. Trade Union Series, no. 6. London: Labour Research Department and George Allen & Unwin, 1920. 244 pp.
    Drake's book is frequently referred to as the standard work on the subject. It remains an excellent source despite its publication date. Although the focus of the book is on the period following World War I, the first section, "The Women's Trade Union Movement," is an excellent account of this activity in the nineteenth century. Lewenhak's book (<u>see</u> entry 170) supplements but does not supersede it. Drake concentrates on the politics of organization, while Lewenhak is more interested in personalities.

79 DYHOUSE, CAROL. "Working-Class Mothers and Infant Mortality in England, 1895-1914." <u>Journal of Social History</u> 12 (1978):248-67.

The question of whether a relationship existed between
high infant mortality and working mothers was a subject
that received a great deal of attention in the first decade
of this century. Dyhouse points out some of the vested
interests who wished to find a positive relationship, including men's trade unions and those who endorsed a middle-
class view of the proper family life. Organizations such
as the Fabian Women's Group and the Women's Industrial
Council defended women's right to work. Little attention
was given to nutrition of mothers and infants. Dyhouse
states the need for further research into methods of infant
care.

80   EBERY, MARK, and PRESTON, BRIAN. Domestic Service in Late
     Victorian and Edwardian England, 1871-1914. Geographical
     Papers, no. 42. Reading, Pa.: Department of Geography,
     University of Reading, 1976. 117 pp.
        The statistics compiled here on domestic service are
     useful, but the authors have applied no imagination in
     interpreting them so the conclusions are uninteresting.
     Footnotes are marred by a high incidence of misspelled
     names, which may make the pursuit of references difficult.

81   ECCLES, CHARLOTTE O'CONNOR. "The Experiences of a Woman
     Journalist." Blackwood's Magazine 153 (1893):830-38.
        This firsthand account describes the struggles of a
     woman to enter the field of journalism in London.

82   ELMY, ELIZABETH C. WOLSTENHOLME. Woman's Franchise: the Need
     of the Hour. 2d ed. London: International Labour Party,
     1907. 14 pp.
        Elmy argues that establishment of a minimum wage for
     women implies acceptance of the idea that their earnings
     can be lower than men's, and will result in insufficient
     income for widows with children and excessive income for
     single men.

83   "Enquirers into Women's Work." Englishwoman's Review 30
     (1899):14-18.
        Women workers, the article argues, would have a stronger
     competitive position in the labor market if they had more
     technical training; improvement of working conditions would
     follow. Anonymous complaints to factory inspectors have
     not accomplished their purpose. Studies of women's and
     children's work are faulted as uneven in quality and
     unsatisfactory.

84   No entry.

85   FAWCETT, MILLICENT GARRETT. "Mr. Sidney Webb's Article on
     Women's Wages." Economic Journal 2 (1892):173-76.

Mrs. Fawcett's response to Webb's article argues that wages depend upon the laborer's power to find other employment at higher wages; therefore training is most important for women to improve their position in competition for higher wages.

86 _____. Review of James Ramsay Macdonald, ed., Women in the Printing Trades. Economic Journal 14 (1904):295-99.
    Fawcett criticizes the book (see entry 184) for representing only the trade union viewpoint, which is hostile to women.

87 _____. What I Remember. London: T. Fisher Unwin, 1924. 271 pp.
    A strong suffragist and leader of the nonmilitants over many years, Fawcett brings some shrewd political observation and a sense of humor to the writing of her autobiography. She and her colleagues, "ladies" and professional women, devoted enormous energy and patience to the suffrage movement. (See also Ray Strachey, entry 274.)

88 _____. Women's Suffrage: a Short History of a Great Movement. London: T. C. & E. C. Jack, 1911. 94 pp.
    _____. The Women's Victory--and After: Personal Reminiscences 1911-1918. London: Sidgwick & Jackson, 1920. 176 pp.
    The first volume, published before the vote had been won, offers a closely argued case for women's suffrage and for the nonmilitant approach. The optimistic tone of its conclusion is amazing, considering the number of years Fawcett had been involved in the struggle. The second volume continues the story, providing a thorough political history, more detailed than that provided in her autobiography (see entry 87).

89 FORD, ISABELLA O. Industrial Women and How to Help Them. London: Humanitarian League, 1894. 12 pp.
    Philanthropists are wrong in teaching women workers patience and acceptance. Working women should be encouraged to take responsibility for their own lives, to bring about reform and improved working conditions by their own efforts. They need to have the vote and freedom to act. This hortatory and idealistic tract presents an interesting point of view.

90 _____. Women as Factory Inspectors and Certifying Surgeons. Investigation Papers, no. 4. Manchester: Women's Co-operative Guild, 1898. 8 pp.
    The advantage of women factory inspectors is that women workers find it easier to approach them than men. A similar argument for women as certifying surgeons (inspecting young workers to see if they are fit to work) is offered. Ford

reiterates her argument in favor of women's trade unions that are powerful enough to insist on law enforcement.

91   _____. Women's Wages and the Conditions Under Which They are Earned. Humanitarian League's Publications, no. 8. London: William Reeves, 1893. 17 pp.

Briefly and with examples, Ford outlines how women's wages are cut and their hours increased, and describes unsatisfactory, unhealthy working conditions experienced by factory and home workers and by shop assistants. Her remedy: "We must teach these women to rebel and not to submit. We must arouse them to a better knowledge of their own work, their own infinite value. . . . We must show them it is one of the most selfish of crimes to submit to injustice, since each of these submissions adds a link to the chain of slavery fettering all working women, not in England only, but all over the world . . ."

92   FRANK, PETER. "Women's Work in the Yorkshire Inshore Fishing Industry." Oral History 4 (1976):57-72.

Wives and daughters of Yorkshire fishermen gathered mussels and limpets for bait, prepared them and baited the lines, and did other physically arduous jobs. The division of labor was based on relative danger rather than the need for strength. Women also salted fish and hawked it in neighboring towns. This is an interesting example of a family-centered cooperative occupation.

93   FRANKLIN, JILL. "Troops of Servants: Labour and Planning in the Country House, 1840-1914." Victorian Studies 19 (1975):211-39.

Architectural plans for houses in England after 1870 show a decline in the extent and elaborateness of servants' quarters, apparently related to a reduction in the size of the staff. Labor saving is a consideration in planning; modern devices, including electric lights, make maintenance simpler. Franklin bases her findings on a few examples; other writers have found that many employers were unconcerned with buying labor-saving devices for their servants.

94   FULFORD, ROGER. Votes for Women. London: Faber & Faber, 1957. 343 pp.

This excellent history of the suffrage movement is helpful in identifying and characterizing the participants. Fulford concludes that the militants delayed things.

A Biographical Index provides brief information about a number of women.

95   GALTON, FRANK W., ed. Workers on Their Industries. London: Swann Sonnenschein, 1895. 239 pp.

During the fall and winter of 1893-94, a series of lectures on "Industries" was presented at the South Place

Institute. Speakers, selected for their practical knowledge of their trades, emphasized union organization in the
lectures, which are brief, not technical, and generally of
high quality. Women's occupations represented are dressmaking (Frances Hicks, secretary of the Women's Trade Union
League), gold and silver polishing (W. Augustus Steward),
agriculture (Frederick Verinder), and pottery (S. J. Thomas).
Emily Holyoake of the Women's Trade Union League contributed
a lecture on "The Need of Organisation of Women."

96   GARLAND, CHARLES H. "Women as Telegraphists." Economic
     Journal 11 (1901):251-61.
         Women telegraphists are reported by their supervisors to
     do routine work well; they are paid 25% less than men, are
     absent from work more often, and tire more easily. Women
     hold supervisory jobs (mainly over other women). Garland
     concludes that women function about as well as men but
     finds that they are more "docile," being less involved in
     labor struggles.

97   GATHORNE-HARDY, JONATHAN. The Unnatural History of the Nanny.
     New York: Dial Press, 1973. 350 pp. Published in Great
     Britain as The Rise and Fall of the British Nanny. London:
     Hodder, 1972.
         Relying heavily on autobiography, novels, and interviews
     of people brought up by nannies, Gathorne-Hardy produces
     some psychological theories about the effect of the nanny
     system on children, especially males. Along the way there
     is discussion of nannies, their background, training, place
     in the household (powerful, in his view), and daily routine.
     He leans toward the sensational. Interviews included eight-
     een with nannies and sixteen with former children, but gen-
     erally his sympathies and interests seem to lie with the
     children.

98   GÉRARD, CLAIRE [pseudo.]. "Les Industries Féminines Anglaises
     et la Lutte Contre le Chômage." Le Musée Sociale, Paris.
     Memoires et Documents, 1900, pp. 133-68.
         A French observer studies what is being done about
     women's employment in England, especially the labor ex-
     changes and the workrooms set up by middle-class women to
     provide work in off seasons.

99   GISSING, GEORGE. The Odd Women. London: Thomas Nelson,
     1907. 479 pp.
         In this novel Gissing explores the difficulties of women
     who live independently; a pair of enterprising feminists
     run a training school for young women with the goal of
     helping them, in turn, be independent and avoid being
     forced to marry for a livelihood. Two pathetic sisters,
     unexpectedly left with insufficient resources, struggle to

maintain themselves. A young woman, finding shop work
tedious, marries to escape and is doomed to a miserable
life.

100 _____. Thyrza, a Tale. 3 vols. London: Smith, Elder & Co.,
1887. Reprint. Brighton: Harvester, 1974. With introduction by Jacob Korg.
    Thyrza and her sister are working girls in Lambeth.
Egremont, a social reformer, comes into their neighborhood
to lecture to working men on literature; he and Thyrza have
a benighted romance. The novel's description of life in
Lambeth, and a highly critical attitude towards the intellectual social reformers and the damage they can do, provide
interesting material.

101 GORE-BOOTH, EVA. "The Movement Among Trade Unionists." In
The Case for Women's Suffrage, edited by Brougham Villiers.
London: T. Fisher Unwin, 1907, pp. 50-65.
    "The vicious circle of political disability working it-
self out in industrial weakness and social impotence" can
be broken only if women have the vote.

102 GORSKY, SUSAN R. "Old Maids and New Women: Alternatives to
Marriage in Englishwomen's Novels, 1847-1915." Journal of
Popular Culture 7 (1973-74):68-85.
    Tracing changes in the possibilities allowed to unmarried
fictional women, Gorsky finds some wider opportunities for
the "new woman," but marriage is still considered the more
desirable alternative in nearly all cases.

103 GREAT BRITAIN. BOARD OF TRADE. Labour Gazette. 1893-1917.
    This publication provides monthly statements of the
Women's Employment Bureau. There are also reports on employment by industry (but not by sex), on legal cases in-
volving workers, and on occupational diseases.

104 _____. _____. Report by Miss Collet on the Statistics of
Employment of Women and Girls. Parliamentary Papers, 1894,
lxxxi, part 2, C.7564.
    Comparing statistics from the 1881 and 1891 censuses,
Collet finds the proportion of women employed remained
stationary, but some changes occurred: fewer married or
elderly women and more women under twenty-five were employed; more middle-class women worked. In the North the
demand for workers was greater than the supply, so employment of women did not drive wages down as it appeared to do
in the South. The report pays particular attention to married women in the work force and to the textile industry.

105 _____. _____. Report on Changes in the Employment of Women
and Girls in Industrial Centres. Part I. Flax and Jute

Centres. By C. E. Collet. Parliamentary Papers, 1898, lxxxviii, C.8794.

With the object of presenting "such official statistics and information with regard to important industrial centres as may throw light on the present industrial position of women in those centres and on the differences among different localities in this respect," this report gives the history of the industry since 1835, changes in population, and wages rates in the districts. Other information includes not only statistics but attitudes of men and women, surplus of women, and effect of low employment of men.

106 GREAT BRITAIN. CHIEF INSPECTOR OF FACTORIES AND WORKSHOPS. Annual Reports. Parliamentary Papers, 1912-13, xxv, Cd.6239; 1914, xxix, Cd.7491.

The reports of the Principal Lady Inspector, included in the Chief Inspector's report, cite the investigations of Lady Inspectors (who are mentioned by name) into complaints about sanitation, poisoning, and accidents, Truck Act violations, hours of labor, and other problems. The 1911 report was Adelaide Anderson's fifteenth. The 1913 report stated: "The women and girls at last begin to press their claims for a better life . . . not only by increasing appeals to inspectors to put the law in motion, but also by criticism of the limitations of the law and by signs of fresh courage in organising and voicing their needs to the employers" (p. 70).

107 GREAT BRITAIN. ROYAL LABOUR COMMISSION. Reports on the Employment of Women by the Lady Assistant Commissioners. Parliamentary Papers, 1893-94, xxxvii, C.6894.

These regional reports give detailed information on trades in which women and girls are employed. Eliza Orne, Clara E. Collet, May E. Abraham, and Margaret H. Irwin gathered the information by statistical research and personal interviews.

108 GREENWOOD, M. "Women in Dust Yards." Englishwoman's Review 31 (1900):158-61.

A description of the happy, healthy lives of the dustwomen who sorted trash.

109 GREENWOOD, WALTER. There Was a Time. London: Cape, 1967. 254 pp.

Greenwood's recollections of his boyhood in Manchester in the early years of the twentieth century include observations on how his mother and other women kept the family finances going by working as waitresses and laundresses, and borrowing from the pawnshop.

110 GREGG, HILDA C. "The Medical Woman in Fiction." Blackwood's Magazine 164 (1898):94-109.

This review essay considers a group of novels about women physicians.

111   GURNHAM, RICHARD. <u>A History of the Trade Union Movement in</u>
      <u>the Hosiery and Knitwear Industry, 1776-1976: the History</u>
      <u>of the National Union of Hosiery and Knitwear Workers, its</u>
      <u>Evolution and its Predecessors</u>. Leicester: The Union, 1976.
      197 pp.
          In Leicester and Nottingham, the two main centers of the
      hosiery and knitwear industry, there were two women's
      unions, the Seamers and Stichers Union and the Menders
      Society. After 1912 more women were recruited into the
      men's unions, but Gurnham finds that women resisted re-
      cruitment and were apathetic as members. Gurnham's account
      of the women's union is brief (he says there is little ma-
      terial available) and he adopts a common male trade-unionist
      view of women as a "problem . . . taking work traditionally
      reserved for men, and usually at substantially lower rates."
      A study concentrating on women workers in this industry
      might yield some interesting results. Bibliography.

112   . GWYNN, STEPHEN. "Bachelor Women." <u>Contemporary Review</u> 73
      (1898):866-75.
          The author rationalizes the increasing propensity of
      educated women to choose careers rather than marriage as
      being consistent with the British tradition of self-help.

113   HAMILTON, CICELY. <u>Marriage As a Trade</u>. London: Chapman &
      Hall, 1909. 284 pp.
          The assumption that marriage is the only proper occupa-
      tion for women leads to their being undervalued; they are
      taught to be dependent and have no self-respect. Being
      accustomed as wives and mothers to earning only subsistence,
      they accept low wages when they do go out to work. Mar-
      riage and children should be chosen, not compulsory. The
      present situation emphasizes the physical responsibilities
      of women and encourages imitativeness, so that women in the
      arts fail to express their own view.

114   HAMILTON, MARY AGNES. <u>Margaret Bondfield</u>. London: Leonard
      Parsons, 1924. 191 pp.
          Hamilton, an admiring friend, tells the story of
      Bondfield's life and accomplishments in glowing terms (she
      compares Bondfield with Joan of Arc at one point). In this
      biography, written during Bondfield's lifetime, the author
      makes much of the long and intimate friendship between
      Bondfield and Mary Macarthur, yet very little attention is
      paid to this relationship in Hamilton's biography of
      Macarthur (<u>see</u> entry 115), written after Macarthur's death.
      Bondfield's life and associations deserve a serious biog-
      raphy. Unfortunately, Hamilton provided no footnotes, bib-
      liography, or index to help future scholars.

115   ____. Mary Macarthur, a Biographical Sketch. London:
        Leonard Parsons, 1925. 209 pp.
            Mary Macarthur, according to this and other descriptions,
        was the golden girl of the women's trade union movement.
        As a leader in the Women's Trade Union League and founder
        of the National Federation of Woman Workers, she was instru-
        mental in strikes of women workers at Cradley Heath and
        Bermondsey. A compelling speaker, she fought for decent
        wages for women until her death in 1921. One wishes for a
        biography with a better perspective than Hamilton's per-
        sonal recollection, which lacks documentation. (See entry
        114.)

116   ____. Women at Work: a Brief Introduction to Trade Unionism
        for Women. London: Routledge, 1941. 188 pp.
            This is a short history of the women's trade union move-
        ment, valuable for its vivid though brief accounts of strikes
        and working conditions. The period before 1914 is described
        in chapters 1, 2, 4, and 5. Mary Macarthur is the dominant
        figure.

117   ____. "Women's Wages and the Vote." Englishwoman 7
        (July-September 1910):41-47, 139-46.
            "The importance of the vote does not rest upon its direct
        influence upon wages. . . ." Hamilton accepts supply and
        demand as the major determinants of wages. She is in favor
        of protective legislation and trade-unionism, but believes
        that the oversupply of women workers, their low level of
        skills, and "general weakness" limit the degree to which
        they can benefit from union organization.

118   HAMMERTON, A. JAMES. Emigrant Gentlewomen: Genteel Poverty
        and Female Emigration, 1830-1914. London: Croom Helm;
        Totowa, N.J.: Rowman and Littlefield, 1979. 220 pp.
            Distressed gentlewomen in the early nineteenth century
        who emigrated to the colonies as governesses found that
        their work included more housekeeping than similar occupa-
        tions at home; because housework did not carry the social
        stigma that it did in England, it became an accepted occu-
        pation. In Edwardian times, there were training programs
        to prepare emigrating women, who, Hammerton finds, were
        more adaptable than has been thought, with the increased
        independence of life in the colonies as a reward. Strong
        pressure existed to send them to the colonies as a "civi-
        lizing factor" and to become wives and mothers as well.
        Hammerton has gathered material from many sources and
        offers interesting interpretations and a more positive
        view than others have. Bibliography.

119   HARBEN, HENRY D. The Endowment of Motherhood. Fabian Tract
        no. 149. London: Fabian Society, 1910. 23 pp.

The Fabians endorsed a scheme of state subsidy to mothers and babies, as well as midwife and nursing care. The program would reduce infant mortality and later disabilities by improved nutrition and care and enable working mothers to remain at home for a proper rest period at the time of birth. Among Harben's arguments one is unusual: by lowering infant mortality the problem of "superfluous women" would be overcome, since more boys than girls die in infancy.

120   HARPER, CHARLES G. <u>Revolted Woman--Past, Present and to Come</u>. London: Elkin Mathews, 1894. 140 pp.
     An example of a tirade against women in general and the "new woman" in particular, this book argues that women are designed to be wives and mothers, are naturally inferior to men, and should stay home.

121   HARRIS, LILLIAN. <u>Abolition of Overtime for Women</u>. Women's Co-operative Guild, Investigation Papers, no. 2. London: Women's Co-operative Guild, 1896. 8 pp.
     Guild members were urged to study the provisions of the law on overtime and report violations, and thus relieve the employees themselves from doing so.

122   _____. <u>The Treatment of Women Employees in the Co-operative Movement, Being a Report of an Enquiry into the Wages, Hours, and Conditions of Women Working in Co-operative Stores in 1895</u>. London: n.p., 1897. 18 pp.
     Reviewing hours, wages, conditions of work, cleanliness, and other aspects of women's work in cooperative establishments, the study notes such advantages as regular short hours but suggests reforms including a one-week holiday and a minimum wage.

123   HARRISON, AMY. <u>Women's Industries in Liverpool</u>. London: Williams & Norgate, 1904. 64 pp.
     A study of the effects on women workers of legislation restricting the hours worked finds, for the most part, no adverse effects. In some industries all workers' hours were reduced; in some, men did the necessary overtime on women's jobs, but this was an expensive solution. Small factories had the most difficulty complying with the new regulations, but since they also offered the worst working conditions Harrison considers it better for them to go out of business. Information is provided on number of women workers, percent of married women, age groups, and wages in the varied industries of Liverpool that included the manufacture of cotton, tobacco, food, paper products, clothing, soap, matches, printing, and bookbinding.

124 HARRISON, BRIAN. "For Church, Queen and Family: the Girls'
     Friendly Society 1874-1920." Past and Present 61 (1973):
     107-38.
          The Girls' Friendly Society was founded in 1874, to
     bring together respectable young working girls under the
     "maternal" influence of the Anglican ladies who sponsored
     it. Workhouse girls, clerks, and domestic servants were
     members in different departments (in 1906 50 percent were
     servants). The Society published three periodicals and
     many pamphlets. Its values were conservative, with empha-
     sis on obedience and neatness. It was strongest in country
     areas. The democratization of society and the growth of
     state welfare services decreased the appeal of membership.
     Harrison points out the benefits to the lady "associates"
     of the society and the value of interaction between classes.

125 _____. Separate Spheres: the Opposition to Women's Suffrage
     in Britain. New York: Holmes & Meier, 1978. 274 pp.
          "The antis," mentioned in passing and usually with a
     sneer in histories of the suffrage movement, receive a
     thoughtful and objective treatment. Harrison analyses the
     people in the antisuffrage movement and the political con-
     ditions that made it possible for them to hold off women's
     suffrage for so long. The bibliographical note gives use-
     ful comments on sources.

126 HASLAM, JAMES. "Female Labour in the Potteries." English-
     woman 3 (July-September 1909):61-73.
          The hazards of lead poisoning in the potteries are
     brought to the attention of the consumer, who is urged to
     insist on pottery with lead-free glazes. For a more de-
     tailed description of the manifestations of lead poisoning,
     see Oliver, Dangerous Trades, entry 227.

127 _____. "Sweating in the Irish Linen Industry." Englishwoman
     9 (January-March 1911):137-46.
          Home-work conditions of Belfast women who make linen
     goods (handkerchiefs, etc.) are described.

128 _____. "Women Workers in the Linen Industry." Englishwoman
     9 (January-March 1911):32-40.
          Haslam describes the working conditions and wages of
     Belfast linen weavers and urges women readers to bring
     pressure to bear to improve their situation.

129 HEATHER-BIGGS, ADA. "The Wife's Contribution to Family Income."
     Economic Journal 4 (1894):51-58.
          A defense of home-work for women on the grounds that
     women have always worked in the home, but their work has
     been considered part of their husbands' production.

130   HEWITT, MARGARET. Wives and Mothers in Victorian Industry.
      London: Rockcliff, 1958. 245 pp.
          Hewitt's thorough study of married women's work concludes
      from available evidence that it was not a bad thing for the
      family except when there was a very young baby. Most mar-
      ried women worked out of necessity, not boredom; in the
      Potteries and the textile towns, many women were the prime
      wage-earners for their families. Bibliography.

131   HIGGS, MARY. "Housing of the Women Workers." Progress 4
      (1909):167-74. "Women's Lodging Homes in London."
      Progress 6 (1911):248-55. "A Visit to the Manchester
      Municipal Women's Lodging House." Progress 8 (1913):163-68.
          In a series of articles, Higgs explores housing for
      women industrial workers who have very little money. She
      describes the unsanitary and sometimes immoral conditions
      of private lodging houses and endorses the idea of munici-
      pal lodgings. The last article describes her firsthand
      experience in a model house in Manchester.

132   HIGGS, MARY, and HAYWARD, E. E. Where Shall She Live? The
      Homelessness of the Woman Worker. London: P. S. King,
      1910. 216 pp.
          Disguised as a tramp, Higgs travelled about the country
      to learn about conditions of lodging for women vagrants.
      Her experiences are included as background for this study
      that also investigated living accommodations for women with
      very small earnings who lived in lodgings paid for weekly.
      The book urges establishment of municipal lodging houses,
      greater government control of common lodging houses, and
      opportunities for women lodgers to participate in making
      these facilities more homelike. Nine appendixes, includ-
      ing a "List of Safe Lodging Homes" (most of them sponsored
      by YWCA, church, or Salvation Army).

133   HOBHOUSE, EMILY. "Dust-Women." Economic Journal 10 (1900):
      411-20.
          Dust-women sorted rubbish; some items, such as glass
      and rags, were recycled. Occasionally a treasure was
      found--money, a glove. Although working conditions varied.
      among the yards (some offered shelter from the weather and
      other amenities), this Women's Industrial Council report
      concludes that it was generally healthy, outdoor work; its
      main disadvantages resulted from the long hours away from
      home, which led to poor housekeeping and neglected children.
      Increasing use of machines threatened the women's jobs.
      This is one of the few works on this occupation, with its
      paradoxical "treasure hunt" aspect that makes it interest-
      ing and unusual.

134   HOBSBAWM, E. J. "Custom, Wages, and Work-Load in Nineteenth-
       Century Industry." In Essays in Labour History, rev. ed.,
       edited by Asa Briggs and John Saville, pp. 113-39. London:
       Macmillan, 1967.
          Both employers and workers learned something about wages
       and labor in this period. Employers learned that labor-
       intensive work was more productive than labor-extensive,
       and began to practice scientific management, schedule
       shorter hours of work, and offer incentives. Workers
       learned "the rules of the game": to demand what the
       traffic would bear, to measure effort by payment (although
       workers' self-respect often was undermined by this tech-
       nique), and to think of their labor as a commodity to be
       sold.
          Although Hobsbawm specifically excludes women and chil-
       dren "since their rate was normally fixed in relation to
       the male wage," changes in men's working conditions obvi-
       ously had implications for women workers.

135   HOGG, EDITH F. "The Fur-Pullers of South London." Nineteenth
       Century 42 (1897):734-43.
          The fur-pullers were home-workers who pulled the fur
       from rabbit skins. Poor ventilation caused respiratory
       disease; the author advocated relocating the work to a
       factory setting where ventilation could be controlled.

136   HOLCOMBE, LEE. Victorian Ladies at Work; Middle-Class Working
       Women in England and Wales 1850-1914. Hamden, Conn.:
       Archon Books, 1973. 253 pp.
          Teachers, nurses, shop assistants, clerks, and civil
       servants are included. The development of teaching and
       nursing into professions and the problems of trade union
       organization in these areas are examined in this thorough
       work.

137   HOLDSWORTH, ANNIE E. Joanna Traill, Spinster. London:
       Heinemann, 1894. 208 pp.
          As a favor to a male settlement-worker friend, Joanna
       takes in a young girl he has rescued from prostitution.
       The novel offers views on philanthropy and on the stigma
       of prostitution in the context of a rather melodramatic
       story.

138   HOLLIS, PATRICIA. "Working Women." History 62 (1977):439-45.
          This bibliographic essay evaluates recent work on British
       working women and points out areas of study that have not
       been adequately examined.

139   "Home Work in the Boot Trade: Notes Communicated By a Per-
       sonal Observer." National Union of Woman Workers. Occa-
       sional Paper, no. 11 (July 1898), pp. 11-13.

The writer deplores the "invasion" of an agricultural village by shoemaking factories, which distribute most of their work to home-workers. "Home work results in: irregularity of habit, idleness, loafing, irresoluteness and aimlessness of character; great variation of wages, due to above irregularity rather than fluctuation of trade; the desire to see every novelty; laxity of housewifery; grasp of coppers and neglect of duty; irregularity, unpunctuality, uncleanliness and untidiness in school children."

140 HORN, PAMELA. Labouring Life in the Victorian Countryside. Dublin: Gill & Macmillan, 1976. 292 pp.
      Not only work, but family life, school, religion, the workhouse, and holidays are discussed. Women's occupations include agricultural work and cottage industries such as straw plaiting and lace making. Appendixes include sample budgets for 1893-94 and a document about female bondagers (farm workers) from the Munby Diaries. The bibliography includes references to collections of manuscripts.

141 _____. The Rise and Fall of the Victorian Servant. Dublin: Gill & Macmillan, 1975. 221 pp.
      This is a thorough, well-written study of the structure of households of various sizes from one servant to three hundred, the hierarchies, duties and social relationships, and attitudes of employers. Horn finds that in general employers were distant, unsympathetic, suspicious, and even fearful of their servants. The employer who took a parental responsibility for young servants does not appear here.
      Appendixes include information on wages and duties, reminiscences, an example of household rules for servants, and an employer's diary. A source heavily relied on is Hannah Cullwick, the servant who became Mrs. Arthur Munby.

142 HUTCHINS, B. LEIGH. Conflicting Ideals: Two Sides of the Woman's Question. London: Thomas Murby, 1913. 83 pp.
      Women need not to be helplessly dependent; society needs to use their brains and skills; and mothers are essential. Hutchins attempts a theoretical, nonpartisan outline of the question, with emphasis on educated women.

143 _____. "The Employment of Women in Paper Mills." Economic Journal 14 (1904):235-45.
      Although employment of women in paper mills did not decline as a result of legislation limiting the hours they could work, they were restricted to certain jobs and could not become journeymen.

144 _____. Home Work and Sweating; the Causes and the Remedies. Fabian Tract no. 130. London: Fabian Society, 1907. 19 pp.

Government regulations to ensure payment of a "living wage" and inspection of workplaces for health hazards are advocated in this tract. Some home-workers would be put out of work under such regulation, but it was seen as necessary for the general good.

145 _____. "Some Aspects of Women's Life and Work." Women's Trades Union Review, no. 74 (July 1909), pp. 6–12.
Citing statistics on women who never marry or who are widowed, Hutchins urges involvement of women in trade unions. The number of widows, she argues, suggests the need for protective legislation for men as well as for women and children.

146 _____. Women in Modern Industry. London: G. Bell & Sons, 1915. 315 pp.
This basic history of women's work begins in the pre-industrial period, but its main concerns are women's work in industry, women in trade unions, and the effects of the Factory Acts. In Lancashire, where women were included in the union with men, they failed to participate actively in union management and committee work; Hutchins speculates that they lacked experience with associations of any kind, and predicted that working in factories would eventually cure that. She analyzed the relationship between the labor movement and the women's movement, with their different origins and sometimes conflicting goals. A chapter on women's wages was contributed by J. J. Mallon.

147 _____. The Working Life of Women. Fabian Tract no. 157. Fabian Women's Group Series, no. 1. London: Fabian Society, 1911. 14 pp.
Population statistics demonstrate the fact that women must work: they outnumber men, and they live longer. They move back and forth, however, between the paid workforce and housework, between "value-in-use" (paid in wages) and "value-in-exchange" (paid in provision of home, security, etc.). They remain unskilled and are not encouraged to think of their work as anything but short-term occupation. Women's work at home should be defined as service to the state; widows with children should be supported by family allowances.

148 HUTCHINS, B. LEIGH, and HARRISON, AMY. A History of Factory Legislation. 3d ed. Preface by Sidney Webb. London: P. S. King, 1926. Reprint. London: Frank Cass & Co., 1966. 298 pp.
The writers, advocates of protective legislation for women, find no evidence that men have replaced women in jobs as a result of such legislation. They are in favor of further regulation of laundries and of home-work. Bibliography.

149   "The International Congress of Women." Englishwoman's Review
      30 (1899):153-62.
         This thorough report on the 1899 Congress describes it
      as dealing with too many topics, but laying a good founda-
      tion for the future. Particular praise is given to a paper
      by Baroness Alexandra Gripenburg advocating improved train-
      ing for women workers in preference to protective legislation.

150   The International Council of Women of 1899. 7 vols. Edited
      by the Countess of Aberdeen. London: T. Fisher Unwin,
      1900.
         The third congress of the International Council of Women
      was held in London in 1899. The sessions, reported in
      these volumes, were concerned with women in the professions,
      education, politics, industry, and social life (philan-
      thropy). Although the papers are uneven in quality, the
      breadth of the discussion offers a view of women's work in
      Britain and elsewhere. Lively debates took place on pro-
      tective legislation for women workers and on home-work, and
      a session on "The Ethics of Wage Earning," which included
      the questions of unpaid housework, equal pay, and minimum
      wage, drew such a crowd that it had to be repeated for a
      second audience.
         Each volume is thoroughly indexed. The volume entitled
      "Report of Council Transactions" contains a list of offi-
      cial delegates and a schedule of meetings.

151   IRWIN, MARGARET H. Home Work in Ireland: Report of an Inquiry
      Conducted for the Scottish Council for Women's Trades. 2d
      ed. Glasgow: The Council, 1913. 151 pp.
         A study of shirtmakers and the problem of decreasing
      piece rates includes a table of information on 149 women
      workers.

152   _____. Women's Work in Tailoring and Dressmaking: Report of
      an Inquiry Conducted for the Scottish Council for Women's
      Trades. Glasgow: The Council, 1900. 37 pp.
         Women worked at less skilled jobs such as making vests
      and trousers; their wages were lower than men's even when
      they performed the same work. The union was less hostile
      to women than it had been. Irwin offers tables of wages
      and family situations, and detailed notes on 70 cases. A
      separate section is devoted to dressmakers.

153   JERMY, LOUISE. Memories of a Working Woman. Norwich: Goose
      & Son, 1934. 188 pp.
         Louise Jermy was born in Hampshire in 1877; her autobiog-
      raphy extends to the 1920s. As a young girl she was appren-
      ticed to a dressmaker, but later she went into service as a
      maid and cook in Birmingham, London, and elsewhere. She
      writes intelligently and perceptively of her family and her

employers, and how she survived in a life fraught with physical and psychological troubles. Autobiographies of working women are not plentiful, and this is an excellent one.

154   JEUNE, SUSAN ELIZABETH MARY, ed. <u>Ladies at Work: Papers on Paid Employments for Ladies, By Experts in the Several Branches</u>. London: A. D. Innes, 1893. 143 pp.
    Intended to show briefly the scope, training, pleasures, and hardships of various occupations suitable for ladies, these essays vary considerably in quality. Journalism is presented as a field with good opportunity and equal pay. Caroline Latimer's essay on medicine stresses the importance of a sound general education and the advisability of starting private practice in an area where there are family connections to help in getting established. Sophia Lonsdale urges ladies to work as rent collectors in the type of housing for the poor established by Octavia Hill. The essays on the arts are extremely vague. The overall theme is that ladies should be serious about their work and obtain the best possible training.

155   JOINT COMMITTEE ON THE EMPLOYMENT OF BARMAIDS. <u>Women as Barmaids</u>. London: P. S. King, 1905. 58 pp.
    Advocating legal abolition of the occupation of barmaid, this tract points to the job's risks of inebriety and moral temptation.

156   JONES, DORA. "The Cheapness of Women." <u>Englishwoman's Review</u> 40 (1909):235-43.
    Middle-class women who were teachers or office workers were earning 30 shillings or less a week; not enough, Jones said, for a woman of this class to live decently and independently.

157   JONES, G. S. "Working Class Culture and Working Class Politics in London, 1870-1900: Notes on the Remaking of a Working Class." <u>Journal of Social History</u> 7 (1974):460-508.
    Working-class life in London in the late nineteenth century had its own distinctive culture symbolized by the music hall, which drew on that segment of society for its songs and jokes. It was an enclosed and defensive world that resisted interference from other groups. Trade unions in London were in a period of stagnation. In politics, artisan socialism declined, and conservatism based on interest rather than class became more widespread. This is an interesting view of the era's political and cultural climate.

158   JONES, T. SPENCER. <u>The Moral Side of Living-In</u>. London: Shop Assistant Publishing Co., 1907. 39 pp.

Shop owners provided living accommodations for their
workers, claiming that this served to protect young employees; yet Jones finds no "parental" supervision. Girls
who came home late might be locked out all night, and the
houses were often in bad neighborhoods. Young men, for-
bidden to marry, were lonely and were led into temptation.

159   KEATING, P. J. Working-Class Stories of the 1890s. London:
         Routledge & Kegal Paul, 1971. 157 pp.
         This collection of stories that depict working-class
      life includes several about women. Kipling's story,
      "Badalia Herodsfoot," also offers some observations on
      philanthropy among the poor.

160   _____. The Working-Classes in Victorian Fiction. London:
         Routledge & Kegan Paul, 1971. 310 pp.
         Keating analyzes the portrayal of working-class charac-
      ters and life in nineteenth-century fiction, with emphasis
      on the period 1880-1900. His survey encompasses industrial
      and East End novels, romances, sociological observation
      novels, and propaganda novels intended to change middle-
      class and upper-class attitudes and working-class habits.

161   KENEALY, ARABELLA. Dr. Janet of Harley Street. London:
         Digby, Lopp & Co., 1893. 340 pp.
         The title character of this novel is an exemplary person
      described as large, homely, and brave. Her protégé,
      Phyllis Eve, takes refuge with her after running away
      from a wicked husband; Dr. Janet renames the young woman
      Adam and trains her to be a doctor, citing the value of
      true womanliness in the practice of medicine. When the
      husband reappears, Dr. Janet advises him to kill himself
      and, in the throes of delirium tremens, he does.

162   KENNEY, ANNIE. Memories of a Militant. London: Edward
         Arnold & Co., 1924. 308 pp.
         The factory girl from Lancashire who was taken up by the
      Pankhursts tells her version of the suffrage movement. She
      idolized Christabel Pankhurst and believed that her authori-
      tarianism was essential to the success of the movement.
      (See also entries 14, 230, and 231.)

163   KITTERINGHAM, JENNIE. "Country Work Girls in Nineteenth-
         Century England." In Village Life and Labour, edited by
         Raphael Samuel, pp. 73-138. London: Routledge & Kegan
         Paul, 1975.
         The work performed by women and children included farm
      work, lace making, straw plaiting, and glove making.
      Kitteringham's vivid and detailed account also describes
      how the middle-class "respectable" view of country women
      expressed dismay that their work required them to raise
      their skirts or to relieve themselves in the open.

164 KNIGHT, PATRICIA. "Women and Abortion in Victorian and
Edwardian England." History Workshop Journal 4
(Autumn 1977):57-69.
More women used medication or chemical-herbal mixtures
for abortion than used instruments, because medicine was
generally cheaper than the services of a midwife or other
operator. Knight describes various methods. This should
be read in conjunction with McLaren's article on "Women's
Work and the Regulation of Family Size" (see entry 189).

165 Labour Woman. Vol. 1, 1913, Vol. 2, 1914.
The journal of the Women's Labour League, this includes
articles on trade unions, the Labour Party, and suffrage;
plans for simple houses; and personal recollections of work
experience. It seems to be written for an audience of working men's wives rather than working women.

166 LANGLEY, HERBERT HUNT. "The Typists' Sex War." Socialist
Review 3 (1909):308-12.
Concerned that experienced men typists were losing jobs
to women who would accept lower wages, the author advocates
equal pay for equal work as a solution to the problem.

167 "Law and the Laundry." Part 1, "Commercial Laundries," by
Mrs. Bernard Bosanquet, Mrs. Creighton, and Mrs. Sidney
Webb. Part 2, "Laundries in Religious Houses," by Lucy C.
F. Cavendish. Nineteenth Century 41 (January-June 1897):
224-35.
Denouncing the law regulating hours and working condi-
tions in laundries as ineffective, these articles recommend
inspection of laundries, particularly those in penitentiaries.

168 LEE, ALAN J. "The Radical Press." In Edwardian Radicalism
1909-1914: Some Aspects of British Radicalism, edited by
A. J. A. Morris, pp. 47-61. London: Routledge & Kegan
Paul, 1974.
This detailed analysis of radical newspapers, their
owners, and editors is useful for researchers using newspapers as source material.

169 LEONARD, JIM. "Lady Bell and Edwardian Middlesbrough." North
East Group for the Study of Labour History Bulletin 8
(1974):5-9.
A social historian looks at Florence Bell's 1907 study,
At the Works. He praises Lady Bell's description of the
workers' homes; she accepts slum development as inevitable,
and ignores trade union organization and local working-class
politics. On the whole he finds that the book is still
useful today.

170   LEWENHAK, SHEILA. <u>Women and Trade Unions, an Outline History</u>
      <u>of Women in the British Trade Union Movement</u>. London:
      Ernest Benn, 1977. 307 pp.
         Women's activity in labor organization from medieval
      times to 1975 is given a brisk but interesting treatment.
      Chapters 5 through 9 are concerned with the late nineteenth
      and early twentieth centuries. Brief biographical informa-
      tion on major women organizers is included. Lewenhak claims
      that the periods when women showed little interest in union
      organization coincided with those when, because of economic
      conditions and employer pressure, men were also inactive.
      <u>See</u> Barbara Drake, <u>Women in Trade Unions</u> (1920), entry 78.

171   LEWIS, ELIZABETH. "A Reformation of Domestic Service."
      <u>Nineteenth Century</u> 38 (January–June 1893):127–38.
         The middle-class housewife burdened with overseeing the
      work of her servants was constantly interrupted in any
      other pursuit. Lewis proposed centralized household ser-
      vice: a neighborhood cooking service to supply meals, and
      an "army" of cleaners. This is one example of the theoriz-
      ing about professionalization and centralization of domestic
      services outside the individual household which was popu-
      lar in the 1890s.

172   LIDDINGTON, JILL, and NORRIS, JILL. <u>One Hand Tied Behind Us,</u>
      <u>the Rise of the Women's Suffrage Movement</u>. London: Virago,
      1978. 304 pp.
         The radical suffragists of Lancashire were textile work-
      ers and other working women who had learned about organiza-
      tion in the union and in the Women's Co-operative Guild.
      The authors, painstakingly digging from a variety of sources
      including oral history interviews, have pieced together the
      story of a strong working-class suffragist group and its
      relationship with trade unions, the Labour Party, and the
      Pankhursts' Women's Social and Political Union. Substan-
      tial background material is provided on women's work and
      family life in Lancashire, as is an impressive amount of
      biographical information on the central figures. The book
      is a fine example of imaginative use of hard-to-find re-
      sources to reconstruct a chapter of history previously
      overlooked. An excellent bibliography with references to
      archival sources and unpublished theses as well as printed
      materials is included.

173   <u>Life in the Laundry</u>. Fabian Tract no. 112. London: Fabian
      Society, 1902. 15 pp.
         The tract advocates regulation of hours and conditions
      of work in laundries by including them in the Factory Acts.
      Working conditions in small establishments are described.
      Charitable organizations and prisons were exempt from in-
      spections and could therefore employ inmates for long hours

under unhealthy conditions, thus competing unfairly with
other laundries.

174   LIVERPOOL WOMEN'S INDUSTRIAL COUNCIL. Report on Home Work in
       Liverpool. Liverpool: The Council, 1908. 80 pp.
           The report of an investigation by Miss E. Mahler,
       Miss C. Phelps, and Miss E. F. Rathbone into home-work in
       tailoring, bootmaking, ready-made clothes, and other manu-
       facture. The main portion is a table of 204 cases. It was
       intended to be used with similar reports from London and
       Glasgow in relation to proposed legislation.

175   LOANE, M. The Common Growth. London: Edward Arnold, 1911.
       304 pp.
       _____. An Englishman's Castle. London: Edward Arnold, 1909.
       308 pp.
       _____. From Their Point of View. London: Edward Arnold,
       1908. 309 pp.
       _____. The Next Street But One. London: Edward Arnold, 1905.
       309 pp.
       _____. The Queen's Poor: Life as They Find It in Town and
       Country. London: Edward Arnold, 1905. 312 pp.
           A district nurse's anecdotes and observations about her
       poor patients and their families provide material that is
       often perceptive, sometimes sentimental, but of interest
       for its picture of the nurse's work and of family life
       among the poor. The author criticizes home industries
       ("the destruction of the home"), has sharp words for dil-
       ettante philanthropists, and urges adequate pay for working
       women.

176   LOW, BARBARA. Some Considerations Concerning Women in the
       Labour Market. London: P. S. King & Son, 1914. 32 pp.
           In a lecture to the National Liberal Club Political and
       Economic Circle, Low acknowledged the problems posed by
       women's position in the labor market and their family ob-
       ligations. Advocating shorter hours and more flexible
       work, she saw a craft system approach (in the home or
       small factory) as a solution. The discussion that followed
       the paper is included.

177   LYTTELTON, EDITH SOPHIE. Warp and Woof, a Play. London:
       T. Fisher Unwin, 1908. 128 pp.
           A play about girls working in a dressmaker's shop, this
       is intended to emphasize the need for enforcement of Fac-
       tory Laws on hours. It was performed in 1904 as a fund-
       raiser for the Industrial Law Society, which spread legal
       information about workers' rights and had an indemnity fund
       for workers who lost their jobs as a result of informing
       the Factory Inspector of violations. Another needleworker,
       the Duchess of York (later Queen Mary), attended a
       performance.

178   LYTTELTON, M. K. <u>Women and Their Work</u>. London: Methuen,
      1901. 152 pp.
           In the context of discussing philanthropy, the profes-
      sions, and other forms of work suitable for educated women,
      Lyttelton stresses the importance of having "conviction."
      Families, especially mothers, should take responsibility
      for teaching their daughters to think clearly and take
      themselves seriously.

179   MACARTHUR, MARY. "The Working of the Trade Boards Act."
      <u>Englishwoman</u> 19 (July-September 1913):270-76.
           The Trade Boards Act is shown to have improved the
      situation of sweated workers, with chain makers, lace
      makers, and tailors as examples. In the long run,
      Macarthur says, healthier people do better work and sweat-
      ing is not an advantage to the employer.

180   McBRIDE, THERESA M. <u>The Domestic Revolution: the Moderniza-</u>
      <u>tion of Household Service in England and France, 1820-1920</u>.
      London: Croom Helm; New York: Holmes & Meier, 1976.
      160 pp.
           Domestic service as an occupation offered geographical
      and social mobility combined with a protected environment
      and work that involved personal relationships. When women
      began to turn away from domestic service, they moved to
      other occupations in which they dealt with people, such as
      clerical and shop work. The experience of employing ser-
      vants taught middle-class women management but it rein-
      forced class divisions. In comparing England and France,
      McBride finds differences in living conditions but simi-
      larities in other aspects. Bibliography.

181   _____. "The Long Road Home: Women's Work and Industrializa-
      tion." In <u>Becoming Visible: Women in European History</u>,
      edited by Renate Bridenthal and Claudia Koontz, pp. 280-95.
      Boston: Houghton Mifflin, 1977.
           Reviewing the evolution of women's work in three phases,
      McBride concentrates on the first (1760-1880) and the tran-
      sition to the second (1880-1940), noting particularly the
      decline in married women's participation in the labor mar-
      ket. She attributes the decline of domestic service to
      employers tiring of dealing with obstreperous servants
      rather than to the servants' desire for independence. Her
      interest is primarily in occupations involving personal
      relationships.

182   McCALL, DOROTHY HOME. "Another Aspect of the Servant Problem."
      <u>National Review</u> 60 (1912):969-73.
           An employer of a small number of servants says she suc-
      ceeds by hiring 14-year-olds and training them herself.
      She claims this method produces good wives and mothers for
      the working classes.

183   MACDONALD, JAMES RAMSAY. <u>Margaret Ethel Macdonald</u>. 4th ed.
       London: Hodder & Stoughton, 1913. 270 pp.
          Margaret Macdonald was active in the Women's Industrial
       Council and instrumental in founding the Women's Labour
       League. She conducted several investigations into women's
       working conditions, and endorsed the need for protective
       legislation for women. Her husband's memoir, written after
       her death at the age of 40, is understandably poetic.

184   MACDONALD, JAMES RAMSAY, ed. <u>Women in the Printing Trades: a
       Sociological Study</u>. London: P. S. King & Son, 1904.
       206 pp.
          Women's work in the printing trades was restricted to
       certain jobs. Women did not join the unions, the study
       concludes, because they thought of their work as temporary
       or did not expect to benefit from the union; on the other
       hand, men did not encourage the women to join. Legislation
       restricting the hours when women might work is found not to
       have inhibited their taking jobs in the printing industry.
       Appendixes include an outline of the enquiry, detailed
       descriptions of typical firms, special reports on Glasgow
       and Birmingham, and wages tables for 1898-99. Investigators
       were Mrs. J. L. Hammond, Mrs. H. Oakeshott, Miss A. Black,
       Miss A. Harrison, and Miss Irwin. For a conflicting opin-
       ion, see Millicent Garrett Fawcett's review of the book
       (entry 86).

185   MACDONALD, MARGARET et al. <u>Wage Earning Mothers</u>. London:
       Women's Labour League, n.d. 32 pp.
          In the early 1900s mothers' work was described as detri-
       mental to children's health and family welfare. In the
       interest of raising healthy citizens for the state an allow-
       ance should be provided for widows with young children, and
       fathers should have assurance of an adequate income.

186   McDOUGALL, MARY LYNN. "Women's Work in Industrializing
       Britain and France." <u>Atlantis</u> 4 (1979):143-51.
          Reviewing recent social and labor histories that focus
       on women in nineteenth century Great Britain and France,
       McDougall finds that the books depict "women as actors in
       history," but that historians of women have not yet grap-
       pled adequately with issues of class.

187   _____. "Working-Class Women During the Industrial Revolution,
       1780-1914." In <u>Becoming Visible: Women in European History</u>,
       edited by Renate Bridenthal and Claudia Koontz, pp. 255-79.
       Boston: Houghton Mifflin, 1977.
          McDougall surveys changes in women's work and social
       role, family life, protective legislation, occupations,
       and trade-union participation in England and France, and
       reviews historical interpretations. A well-selected brief
       bibliography is included.

188   McKIBBIN, ROSS I. "Social Class and Social Observation in
      Edwardian England." <u>Transactions of the Royal Historical
      Society</u>, 5th ser. 28 (1978):175-99.
          McKibbin examines the writings of Mrs. Bosanquet, Miss
      Loane, and Lady Bell as studies of social class through
      personal observation, and attempts to understand social
      classes through "their codes, conventions, habits and
      mental horizons." He presents the problems they studied
      and considers their historiographical importance. He
      praises them for being aware of their own limitations as
      middle-class observers, and is particularly interested in
      their attempts to understand the ways in which the "values
      of one [class] infiltrate those of another."

189   McLAREN, ANGUS. "Women's Work and Regulation of Family Size:
      the Question of Abortion in the Nineteenth Century." <u>His-
      tory Workshop Journal</u> 4 (1977):70-81.
          Women factory workers in nineteenth-century Lancashire
      used abortion as a means of limiting family size. Among
      the middle and upper classes, withdrawal was the accepted
      means; these classes disapproved of abortion. For working-
      class women, abortion had two advantages: the decision on
      whether or not to terminate a pregnancy could be postponed
      for a time, and it was a means controlled by women.

190   MALLET, C. <u>Dangerous Trades for Women</u>. The Humanitarian
      Leagues' Publications no. 9. London: William Reeves,
      1893. 22 pp.
          Symptoms of lead and phosphorus poisoning are described
      in detail in this pamphlet that recommends prohibition of
      the use of these materials in industry. Consumers are
      urged to refuse to buy phosphorus matches or pottery with
      lead-based glazes, and to demand alternatives such as the
      Salvation Army's "Darkest England" matches.

191   MARCH-PHILLIPPS, EVELYN. <u>Evils of Home-work for Women</u>.
      Women's Co-operative Guild Investigation Papers no. 3.
      London: Women's Co-operative Guild, 1898. 7 pp.
          The best cure for the evils is to encumber home-work
      with so much legislation that the employer will cease to
      find it worthwhile.

192   _____. "Factory Legislation for Women." <u>Fortnightly Review</u>,
      o.s. 63, n.s. 57 (1895):733-44.
          This article supports the proposed Factory Acts on the
      grounds that they will improve working conditions for women.

193   _____. "The New Factory Bill: As It Affects Women." <u>Fort-
      nightly Review</u>, o.s. 61, n.s. 55 (1894):738-48.
          The Factory Bill, described as a "pilot," offers hope
      for future improvement. This article gives particular
      attention to problems of laundresses and home-workers.

194 _____. "The Progress of Women's Trade Unions." <u>Fortnightly</u>
   <u>Review</u>, o.s. 60 (1893):92-104.
   The author is optimistic about women's increasingly
   vigorous participation in trade unions, and believes men
   are becoming more willing to include women in union
   activity.

195 MARKHAM, VIOLET R. <u>May Tennant, a Portrait</u>. London: Falcon
   Press, 1949. 72 pp.
   As one of the first two women factory inspectors, May
   Tennant investigated lead hazards, and working conditions
   in linen mills. She left this work to marry a Liberal
   politician and worked with him on labor problems. She was
   Irish, and for recreation she liked to bet on the horses.
   A friend's memoir.

196 MARTIN, ANNA. <u>The Married Working Woman, A Study</u>. London:
   National Union of Women's Suffrage Societies, 1911. 47 pp.
   Drawing illustrations from a working women's club in
   Southeast London at which she worked, the author shows that
   reform by legislation is not solving their problems, and in
   fact is effectively harassing them by inflicting a series
   of measures impossible for them to obey, or by creating
   hardships without compensation (raising school-leaving age,
   making it illegal to bring babies into pubs). She urges
   the vote for these women so they can bring their practical
   experience to bear on the problems. She also advocates a
   minimum wage law.

197 _____. "The Mother and Social Reform." <u>Nineteenth Century</u>,
   1913, pp. 1060-79; 1235-55.
   As long as wives are in the position of functioning as
   their husbands' employees, they have no legal protection.
   Social reform legislation imposes practical difficulties by
   requiring standards of children's education and care without increased income. The mother as "home-maker and therefore as empire builder" deserves adequate compensation.

198 MARTINDALE, HILDA. <u>From One Generation to Another, 1839-1944</u>.
   London: George Allen & Unwin, 1944. 208 pp.
   The author writes about the lives of her mother, her
   sister, and herself. Her mother, Louisa Spicer Martindale,
   was a suffragist and Liberal, active in philanthropic work
   that included organizing a medical dispensary in Brighton
   for women, staffed by women doctors. She was determined
   that her daughters should have careers, Louisa as a doctor,
   Hilda in social service, and saw to it that they were educated for these professions. Louisa, the older, became a
   surgeon (<u>see</u> entry 201). Hilda describes in detail her own
   career as a factory inspector, beginning in 1901. She in-
   spected dressmaking establishments, brickfields, potteries,

and dust yards in England; and laundries and factories in Ireland, as well as violations of the Truck Acts in the Donegal knitting industry. The book is an interesting document of the influence of a career-minded mother on her daughters.

199   _____. Women Servants of the State, 1870-1938; a History of Women in the Civil Service. London: George Allen & Unwin, 1938. 218 pp.

Chapters 1 and 2 describe the entry of women into branches of the civil service before 1914: the Post Office and (after 1904) the Telephone Service employed women for clerical work, as did the National Health Insurance Commission after 1912. Women were employed as Poor Law inspectors as early as the 1870s. The Board of Education had women inspectors, and the Home Office had women factory inspectors. The Labour Department's women investigators included Clara Collet. Martindale stresses the suitability of women for certain types of investigation and inspection. She herself was a factory inspector (see entry 198). Bibliography.

200   MARTINDALE, LOUISA. Under the Surface. Brighton: Southern Publishing Co., 1912. 72 pp.

Martindale seeks to prove that prostitution exists because of women's economic dependence on men. The first step toward independence is the vote. State regulation of prostitution protects men and penalizes women.

201   _____. A Woman Surgeon. London: Victor Gollancz, 1951. 253 pp.

Louisa Martindale's autobiography describes her education, medical training, and practice. Although she seldom mentions dates, her education and early career took place before World War I. Like her sister, Hilda (see entry 198) Louisa gives credit to her mother for starting her on her career.

202   MASON, BERTHA. The Story of the Women's Suffrage Movement. Introduction by the Right Rev. the Lord Bishop of Lincoln. London: Sherratt & Hughes, 1912. 96 pp.

Mason's history begins in the pre-Cromwell period. She obviously finds the militant suffragettes an embarrassment, but explains their actions in terms of the long frustrations of the cause. Her account discusses the activities of Lancashire working women (see entry 172). Like Fawcett and Pankhurst in their 1911 books, she concludes with astonishing confidence of imminent success.

203   MEACHAM, STANDISH. A Life Apart, the English Working Class 1890-1914. Cambridge: Harvard University Press, 1977. 272 pp.

The working class in the years 1890-1914 experienced first a rise, then a fall, in their standard of living; with mechanization a decline in the importance of the skilled worker also occurred. Women's roles, both as factory girls and as working-class wives, changed. In this excellent study, Meacham finds that members of the working class resisted middle-class efforts at social reform, preferring to rely on themselves and their own customs. They feared interference, whether from government or reformers. Bibliography.

204   MEREDITH, MAUD. "Housing of Educated Women Workers." Englishwoman 9 (January-March 1911):159-64.
    To fill the need for housing "without grandmotherly regulations" for professional women, Meredith proposes co-operative housing with catered meals, and possibly child-care centers. The idea of centralization of housekeeping and cooking is offered as a solution to the particular problem of professional women who had little time to spare for such matters.

205   MEYER, ADELE, and BLACK, CLEMENTINA. Makers of Our Clothes: a Case for Trade Boards: Being the Results of a Year's Investigation into the Work of Women in London in the Tailoring, Dressmaking, and Underclothing Trades. London: Duckworth & Co., 1909.   304 pp.
    In 1908, an investigation into the conditions of women's work in London in the tailoring, dressmaking, and under-clothing trades was done at the instigation of the Anti-Sweating League to support advocacy of the Wages Boards bill. The method of study was personal interview with employers and workers. The results compiled here give detailed accounts of how and under what conditions work is performed in these trades. The report is objective, detailed, observant, and perceptive. It shows a wide variety of working conditions and wages. Among interesting conclusions: it is the more secure woman who holds out for decent pay; women's wages are not usually merely supplementary income. The report advocates industrial training schools for women, improved housing, and legal controls of fines, charges, and deductions from wages. Appendixes include the questionnaires and an extensive tabulation of cases with "remarks" of the interviewer. Much detail makes this a useful book.

206   MIDDLETON, LUCY, ed. Women in the Labour Movement: The British Experience. London: Croom Helm; Totowa, N. J.: Rowman & Littlefield, 1977.   221 pp.
    Part 1, "The Early Years" (pp. 15-143), contains six historical essays on women in labor politics; social services (especially those serving children); the Women's

43

Labour League and its contribution to the suffrage movement
(it endorsed full adult suffrage and was nonmilitant);
internationalism (mainly after 1914); the early trade union
years; and the cooperative movement. Organizations discussed include the Women's Labour League, the Women's Protection and Provident League, the Federation of Women
Workers, the Women's Co-operative Guild, and the Trades
Union Congress. The history of women's role in the Labour
Party is particularly well covered, as is the early history
of women's trade union activity. Biographical notes supply
very brief identifications. Bibliography.

207 MITCHELL, HANNAH. The Hard Way Up, the Autobiography of
     Hannah Mitchell, Suffragette and Rebel. Edited by
     Geoffrey Mitchell. Preface by Sheila Rowbotham. London:
     Virago, 1977. 260 pp.
         Hannah Mitchell left her Derbyshire birthplace as a
     young girl and worked as a household servant and as a
     shop girl until she married. She became active in poli-
     tics as a speaker for the International Labour Party and a
     suffragette. Her views on the transition from rural to
     city life, on her experiences at work, and on the difficul-
     ties of combining marriage with political activity are
     stated frankly and with intelligence and humor.

208 MOORE, GEORGE. Esther Waters. London: Walter Scott, 1894.
     377 pp.
         The heroine of this novel works as a servant, has an
     illegitimate child, and later marries its father who dies
     of consumption. The novel emphasizes the insecure condi-
     tion of servants and their reliance on the goodwill of
     their employers.

209 MOORE, MICHAEL J. "Social Work and Social Welfare: the
     Organization of Philanthropic Resources in Britain, 1900-
     1914." Journal of British Studies 16 (1977):84-104.
         Two experiments in social work of the early twentieth
     century, the Guild of Help movement and the Social Welfare
     movement, illustrate different approaches. The Guild, based
     on a German model, combined volunteer casework with commu-
     nity welfare activities. The Social Welfare organizations
     had a larger concept of social work that included the needs
     of all segments of the community; they coordinated services,
     raised money, and campaigned for legislation.

210 MORLEY, EDITH JULIA, ed. Women Workers in Seven Professions:
     a Survey of Their Economic Conditions and Prospects.
     London: George Routledge & Sons, 1914. 318 pp.
         The professions examined are those of teacher, doctor/
     dentist, nurse/midwife, sanitary inspector, civil servant,
     clerk/secretary, and actress. Essays, written by members

of the professions and edited for the Studies Committee of
the Fabian Women's Group, vary in contents and length. One-
third of the book is on teaching: levels, preparation,
salaries, and chance of promotion, with extensive tables
on cost and duration of training courses, scholarships,
prizes, etc. The essay on medicine gives a history of
women in the profession. Those on civil service and secretarial work plead for decent pay and better working conditions. Sanitary inspection, a new occupation for women,
involved enforcement of health regulations; women were considered especially suited to certain duties which required
delicacy and tact. Each essay surveys qualifying requirements (and the cost to acquire them), working hours, time
off, and opportunities for advancement.

211   MUDIE-SMITH, RICHARD, comp. Sweated Industries: Being a
      Handbook of the "Daily News" Exhibition. London: Daily
      News Office, 1906.
        The Sweated Industries Exhibition, designed to arouse
      the public conscience and create pressure for legislation,
      took place in May 1906. The Handbook lists members of the
      Council, exhibits, and lectures; short essays describe
      sweated trades. "Particulars of workers at stalls" gives
      the hours and earnings of the workers on display, the re-
      tail price of the article made, and other information.
      "The attention of visitors is directed to the fact that
      the workers are forbidden to accept any gratuities."

212   MUGGERIDGE, KITTY, and ADAM, RUTH. Beatrice Webb: a Life,
      1858-1943. New York: Alfred A. Knopf, 1968. 271 pp.
        An early interest in social work led Beatrice Potter to
      socialism, Sidney Webb, and the Fabian Society. The extra-
      ordinary partnership of the Webbs produced an astonishing
      quantity of social research and leadership in reform poli-
      tics. This biography tells the story of Beatrice Webb's
      life more succinctly than the several autobiographical
      volumes.

213   MUIRHEAD, M. T. "Report on the Pen Trade in Birmingham."
      Women Workers (Birmingham) 11 (September 1901):34-37.
        Nearly twenty-five percent of women workers in Birmingham
      were employed in pen making, a trade that required dexterity
      but not training; many of the women were married. The Pen
      Workers' Union, formed in 1897, encountered the "usual dif-
      ficulties" of women's unions.

214   _____. "Women Workers in the Printing and Stationery Trades
      in Birmingham." Women Workers (Birmingham) 9
      (September 1901):31-33.
        Muirhead found that women received little training in
      these trades; that the union would not allow women

compositors; and that women performed different jobs from men. Factory legislation was not found to hinder women's employment.

215   MUNBY, ARTHUR J., ed. Faithful Servants: Being Epitaphs and Obituaries Recording Their Names and Services. London: Reeves & Turner, 1891. 400 pp.
      Munby, a barrister, was fascinated with servants (he photographed many and married one). This is a compilation of inscriptions from servants' tombstones; publication of this curiosity says something about nineteenth-century attitudes toward servants.

216   NASH, MRS. VAUGHAN. Reduction of Hours of Work for Women. Women's Co-operative Guild Investigation Papers no. 1. London: The Guild, 1896. 7 pp.
      This includes a comparative analysis of hours of work in several areas including the textile industry.

217   NATIONAL ANTI-SWEATING LEAGUE. Report of Conference on a Minimum Wage, Held at the Guildhall, London. London: Co-operative Printing Society, 1907. 97 pp.
      For three days in October 1906 the National Anti-Sweating League and the London Daily News presented an Exhibition of Sweated Industry to arouse public opinion about the conditions and wages of sweated workers. A conference followed, the purpose of which was to determine a course of action. Sidney Webb presented a theoretical paper, various systems of regulation were advocated, and the question of minimum wage was discussed. Among the participants in the conference were Clementina Black, Magdalen Stuart (Maud Pember) Reeves, Mary Macarthur, and Gertrude Tuckwell. (See also entry 211.)

218   NATIONAL CONFERENCE ON THE UNEMPLOYMENT OF WOMEN DEPENDENT ON THEIR OWN EARNINGS. Women's Industrial News 41 (1907): 669-705.
      In this report of a conference held at London's Guildhall on 15 October 1907, Clementina Black criticized the most frequently suggested remedies for women's unemployment--domestic service and emigration--as solutions unavailable to women with dependents. Margaret Smith reported on Birmingham women in tailor shops and seasonal trades. Margaret Irwin advocated training for skilled work and opening new occupations (such as dairy farming) to women. Miss Wilson of the Boot and Shoe Trade Union, Leicester, spoke about the need for organizing women workers.

219   NATIONAL UNION OF WOMEN WORKERS OF GREAT BRITAIN AND IRELAND. "Women Workers." Papers Read at a Conference, 1891-1918.

The conferences, held in a different city each year, presented papers on themes relating to women's work and issues of interest to women: trade unions, training programs, factory legislation, nursing, teaching, government work, suffrage, temperance, and others. Emphasis and quality vary, and a study correlating the shifts in emphasis with the historical context and the composition of the board of officers would be interesting.

The reports include lists of officers, branches, and members, and reports of committees of the Union and its predecessor, the National Council of Women of Great Britain.

220 No entry.

221 NATIONAL UNION OF WOMEN'S SUFFRAGE SOCIETIES. Women Workers and Women's Votes, n.d.
A series of leaflets addressing various categories of women workers--nurses, teachers, agricultural and industrial women--on the suffrage issue.

222 NEALE, R. S. "Working-Class Women and Women's Suffrage." In Class and Ideology in the Nineteenth Century, pp. 143-68. London and Boston: Routledge & Kegan Paul, 1972.
Neale argues that working-class women had no substantial role in the suffrage movement in England, although they were exploited by the middle-class leaders of the Women's Social and Political Union. For women in unskilled, poorly paid work, and wives of working men, the universal suffrage idea had greater appeal. For another point of view, see Jill Liddington and Jill Norris, One Hand Tied Behind Us (entry 172).

223 NUSSEY, HELEN G. "The Work of a Hospital Almoner." In Methods of Social Advance, edited by C. S. Loch, pp. 18-28. London: Macmillan, 1904.
The hospital almoner determines whether patients are eligible for benefits such as out-patient relief, assistance in obtaining surgical equipment, and home care. She advises patients who are not eligible on how they can manage on their own. Nussey, an almoner herself, gives much emphasis to moral principles and deserving patients.

224 OAKESHOTT, GRACE. "Women in the Cigar Trade in London." Economic Journal 10 (1900):562-72.
Women entered the cigar industry in London after men and children were already established in it. They were paid about twenty-five percent less than men, but gained a foothold. They belonged to the same union as the men and could achieve journeyman status. Evaluating cigar making as a good trade for women, healthy, with reasonable hours, light work, and little pressure, Oakeshott sees women's own lack of a serious attitude as the chief obstacle to their success.

225   "Of the Admission of Women to the Legal Profession: a Word
      in Favour, by a Solicitor." Englishwoman 9
      (January-March 1911):293-300.
         The anonymous author gently reasons that women would do
      no harm to the legal profession and ought to be admitted
      to it.

226   OLCOTT, TERESA. "Dead Centre: the Women's Trade Union Move-
      ment in London, 1874-1914." London Journal 2 (1976):33-50.
         The Women's Trade Union League had a more difficult task
      organizing women in London than in the provinces.   Ini-
      tially, they followed the traditional practice of organiz-
      ing by crafts.   They opposed protective legislation for
      women, and thereby alienated the male leaders of the Trades
      Union Congress.   The union leadership believed in coopera-
      tion among the classes; more radical members broke away to
      form the Women's Trade Union Association.   After 1900,
      especially under Mary Macarthur's leadership, women's un-
      ions were organized to suit women's needs more realisti-
      cally: members could leave while raising children and
      reenter later; the need for protective legislation and for
      male-female unions was accepted.   The result was that by
      1912 they achieved greater success in organizing.

227   OLIVER, THOMAS, ed. Dangerous Trades. London: John Murray,
      1902.   864 pp.
         Doctors, factory inspectors, and others contributed to
      this huge volume on the dangers of various occupations.
      A chapter on infant mortality blames many infant deaths
      on the fact that married women work.   Conditions in home
      laundries, especially where machinery has been introduced,
      are unhealthy and hazardous, and the long hours made women
      rough and hard-drinking.   The dreadful diseases of exposure
      to chemicals in the potteries and match factories are de-
      scribed in lurid detail.   Women migrants doing fish curing
      moved with the herring season; they suffered from long
      hours of work, exposure to the weather, and many cuts and
      sores.   Tinplate workers and bottlers of aerated water,
      many of them women, worked in conditions of risk.   The book
      attempts to be all-encompassing; it includes statistics,
      cures, and recommendations for improvement in a wide vari-
      ety of trades.

228   OREN, LAURA. "The Welfare of Women in Laboring Families in
      England, 1860-1950." In Clio's Consciousness Raised: New
      Perspectives on the History of Women, edited by Mary S.
      Hartmann and Lois Banner. New York: Harper & Row,
      pp. 226-44.
         Drawing on studies such as Magdalen Stuart Reeves's
      Round About a Pound a Week, Oren examines family budgets
      and discusses the difference in expenditures for men, women,

and children. The wife, who managed the household budget,
spent a smaller share on her own nutrition than that of
other members of the family. Because the husband was usually the primary wage-earner, his health was essential to
family welfare.

229 PAINE, WILLIAM. Shop Slavery and Emancipation, A Revolution-
       ary Appeal to the Educated Young Men of the Middle Class.
       Introduction by H. G. Wells. London: P. S. King & Co.,
       1912. 125 pp.
         Exhorting his fellow workers to fight for their rights,
       Paine provides a firsthand description of the working and
       living conditions of men and women shop workers.

230 PANKHURST, SYLVIA. The Suffragette. New York: Sturgis &
       Walton, 1911. 517 pp.

231 _____. The Suffragette Movement. London: Longmans Green &
       Co., 1931. 631 pp.
         In these two volumes Sylvia Pankhurst gives her version
       of the suffragette movement. As the only Pankhurst to
       take strong continuing interest in bringing working-class
       women into the movement, she provides some account of their
       participation and of her work in London's East End organiz-
       ing suffragette activity. Her growing estrangement from
       her sister Christabel and their mother, partly caused by
       her own determination to include working women in the move-
       ment, is evident in the second volume.

232 PAPWORTH, LUCY WYATT, and ZIMMERN, DOROTHY M. Clothing and
       Textile Trades: Summary Tables. London: Women's Indus-
       trial Council, 1912. 12 pp.
         The tables, which focus on wages, are composed of sta-
       tistics on women and girls in the clothing and textile
       trades taken from the 1901 Census, the Inquiry into Produc-
       tion and Inquiry into Earnings and Hours of 1906-07, and
       the Factory Returns of the Home Office.

233 _____. The Occupations of Women According to the Census of
       1911 of England and Wales. Summary Tables. London:
       Women's Industrial Council, 1914.
         Among the useful compilations is a comparative table of
       "Proportions of women in certain occupations for the six
       census years, 1861-1911."

234 PARTICK, M. L. "How I Began to Earn My Living." Labour
       Woman, no. 5, September 1913, pp. 67-68.
         Before she married, Partick worked as a milk carrier,
       apprentice mantle maker, shop girl, and clothing factory
       worker.

235 PEARSON, KARL. "Woman and Labour." <u>Fortnightly Review</u>,
     o.s. 61, n.s. 55 (1894):561-77.
       The problem for women, in Pearson's view, is to recon-
     cile the demands of maternity with the demands of self-
     realization.

236 PETHICK LAWRENCE, EMMELINE. <u>My Part in a Changing World</u>.
     London: Victor Gollancz, 1938. 367 pp.
       A leader of the suffrage movement gives her own account
     of her work in the movement, in social reform, and in settle-
     ment work. She was influenced by William Morris and Edward
     Carpenter, and for her the prime motive for women's suf-
     frage was "the economic and social deliverance of the toil-
     ing masses of the people."

237 PHILIPPS, LEONORA. <u>A Dictionary of Employments Open to Women,</u>
     <u>With Details of Wages, Hours of Work, and Other Information</u>,
     by Mrs. Philipps, assisted by Miss Marian Edwardes, Miss
     Janet Tuckey, and Miss E. Dixon. London: The Women's
     Institute, 1898. 152 pp.
       The compilers attempt to describe all possible occupa-
     tions for women, ranging from the "caller" who goes around
     a poor neighborhood waking people who have no clocks, to
     the doctor. Some of the occupations described had only one
     female incumbent at the time. The tone is open-minded and
     optimistic, although discouraging aspects are not over-
     looked. The extent of information varies; the most detailed
     entries state qualifications, wages, training, and other
     information. An appendix lists training institutes by
     occupation.

238 PHILLIPS, MARION. "What Political Trade Unionism Means to
     Working Women." <u>Labour Woman</u>, no. 1, May 1913, pp. 13-14.
       Phillips's explanation indicates that the protection
     that men's trade unions offer to families is the greatest
     benefit they offer to women.

239 PORTER, G. R. <u>The Progress of the Nation in its Various Social</u>
     <u>and Economic Relations from the Beginning of the Nineteenth</u>
     <u>Century</u>. Revised by F. W. Hirst. London: Methuen, 1912.
     735 pp.
       Porter's book, originally published in 1836, is described
     by Hirst as "a storehouse of information." Hirst brings
     the information up to 1910. It is a compendium of statis-
     tics on wages, rent, diet, communication, trades and occu-
     pations, insurance, crime, and much more.

240 PRATT, EDWIN A. <u>A Woman's Work for Women</u>. London: George
     Newnes, 1898. 132 pp.
       Louisa Hubbard's particular interest was in helping
     middle-class women to find work. Although her career

ended in 1893, she originated a number of ideas that ex-
panded in later years: employment registries, residences
for working ladies, and promotion of occupations such as
midwifery and nursing for educated women. She founded a
journal, the Woman's Gazette, and the Englishwomen's Year-
book. This brief memoir suggests that further research
might be interesting.

241   PROTHERO, ROWLAND E. Women's Suffrage. London: National
      Union of Women's Suffrage Societies, n.d. 13 pp.
         The defense of suffrage offered in this address to a
      reunion of the Women's Suffrage Societies, held at Bedford,
      14 March 1912, is based on the change in women's work and
      the resulting need for power to influence politics and
      trade unions. Prothero argues that women take more inter-
      est in politics and the Empire than men do, and their expe-
      rience in managing household finances makes them more
      intelligent than their husbands.

242   REEVES, MAGDALEN STUART (Maud Pember Reeves). Round About a
      Pound a Week. London: G. Bell & Sons, 1913. Reprint.
      London: Virago, 1979, with an introduction by Sally
      Alexander. 231 pp.
         Personal observation of daily life makes this a vivid
      document of working-class history. Reeves participated in
      a Fabian Women's Group study to determine the effect of
      diet on mothers and children; families in South London with
      a weekly income of 18 to 30 shillings were studied over a
      four-year period. None of the mothers worked outside the
      home except when their husbands were unemployed. There was
      little evidence of help from relatives outside the immedi-
      ate family, but there was a great deal of cooperation among
      neighbors. The introduction describes the work and member-
      ship of the Fabian Women's Group.

243   REINHERZ, H. "The Housing of the Educated Working Woman."
      Englishwoman's Review 31 (1900):7-11.
         Critical of philanthropic efforts to provide housing
      for educated working women so that they can live on their
      substandard wages, the author says such assistance only
      holds down their wages. "What women need today is equality
      before the law and equality of opportunity, the right to
      solve their own problems and fight their own battles. . . ."

244   "Report on the Condition of Female Shop Assistants in London."
      In Women's Industrial Council, Annual Report. 3d ed.
      London: The Council, 1896-97, pp. 17-19.
         This is a synopsis of the full report, which was not pub-
      lished because of lack of funds. It includes information
      on hours, meal times, seats, salaries, fines, rules, food,
      and comfort.

245   "Report on the Millinery Trade." <u>Women's Industrial News</u>,
       n.s. 34 (March 1906):535-41.
           The straw hat and wholesale millinery trade had no real
       apprentice system. Working conditions were good, although
       it was a seasonal trade. Designers and copyists were in
       demand, and advancement to the position of forewoman was
       possible.

246   "Reports on Skilled Employments for Women." <u>Charity Organiza-
       tion Review</u>, n.s. 7 (June 1900):325-28; 8 (July 1900):
       47-49; 9 (February 1901):101-40; 10 (November 1901):
       276-77; 12 (July 1902):54-55.
           These short reports on the conditions of work were writ-
       ten for Charity Organization Society workers, school mana-
       gers, and others engaged in helping young girls select their
       work. Among the occupations considered are bookbinding,
       dressmaking, and work in the jam factory.

247   RIDGE, WILLIAM PETT. <u>Mrs. Galer's Business</u>. London: Methuen,
       1905. 313 pp.
           This novel tells the story of Mrs. Galer's progress from
       her home laundry in Clerkenwell, London, and keeping lodgers,
       to managing her own steam laundry.

248   ROBERTS, ELIZABETH. "Working-Class Standards of Living in
       Barrow and Lancaster, 1890-1914." <u>Economic History Review</u>,
       2d ser. 30 (1977):306-19.
           In the two areas studied, few women worked full-time
       outside the home, but a substantial number earned casual
       wages through occasional employment or home-work. Although
       this factor in the standard of living is not presently quan-
       tifiable, it must be considered; similarly, supplies of
       free or cheap food (gardens, gifts, etc.) and the relative
       proportion of expenditure for housing and drink should be
       considered. Oral history provides a source of information
       in these areas.

249   ROBERTS, ELIZABETH, and LIDDINGTON, JILL. "Working-Class
       Women in the North West (I and II)." <u>Oral History</u> 5
       (1977):7-45.
           Two patterns appear in a pair of studies of married
       women. Married women in Barrow and Lancaster stayed at
       home and took charge of house, children, and family finances.
       In the cotton towns, women weavers continued working and
       earning high wages; they were politically minded, joined
       the unions and the cooperative guilds, and supported the
       demand for women's suffrage. The differences are analyzed
       by Liddington in the second article.

250   ROBERTS, ROBERT. <u>The Classic Slum: Salford Life in the First
       Quarter of the Century</u>. Manchester: Manchester University
       Press, 1971. 219 pp.

251   ____. A Ragged Schooling: Growing Up in the Classic Slum.
         Manchester: Manchester University Press, 1976. 189 pp.
             Roberts's autobiographical account of an Edwardian boy-
         hood provides a picture of how his mother combined running
         a shop with raising a family.

251a   ROBERTSON, JOHN. Report on Industrial Employment of Married
         Women and Infantile Mortality. Birmingham: City of
         Birmingham Health Department, 1910. 27 pp.
             A study based on information collected by health visi-
         tors who observed two hundred mothers in two wards of
         Birmingham during their pregnancies and the first year of
         their babies' lives found no correlation between mothers'
         employment and infant mortality. Robertson speculates that
         decreased likelihood of breast feeding among working mothers
         may be a negative factor, but observes that adequate pre-
         natal nutrition is a positive one.

252   ROBINS, ELIZABETH. The Convert. London: Methuen, 1907.
         359 pp.
             This is a romantic novel woven around an account of the
         militant suffragettes and their meetings; names are changed
         but speeches and incidents are drawn from actual events.

253   ROSEN, ANDREW. Rise Up, Women: the Militant Campaign of the
         Women's Social and Political Union 1903-1914. London and
         Boston: Routledge & Kegan Paul, 1974. 312 pp.
             Rosen's thorough and perceptive history of the Women's
         Social and Political Union points out the early involvement
         and later discarding of working-class women. He believes
         that neither the arson campaign nor the hunger strikes were
         effective and that leaders of the WSPU failed to recognize
         that militant actions of a "relatively small group of
         middle-class women" could not greatly influence the nation's
         politics. Bibliography.

254   ROVER, CONSTANCE. Women's Suffrage and Party Politics in
         Britain, 1866-1914. London: Routledge & Kegan Paul, 1967.
         240 pp.
             This history of the suffrage campaign emphasizes the
         party affiliations of the suffragists and analyzes responses
         of the parties to the issue. At the end of this forceful,
         well-documented book, the author suggests that this episode
         was "a blot on our constitutional history." Bibliography.

255   ROWNTREE, B. SEEBOHM. Poverty: A Study of Town Life. 2d ed.
         London: Macmillan, 1902. 452 pp.
             A landmark study of the life of the poor in York,
         Rowntree's investigation is filled with detail about in-
         come, food, clothing, etc. Rowntree demonstrated that
         severe poverty was not restricted to London, and while

maintaining scientific objectivity, pointed out the physical inadequacy of people who must live on insufficient food and in substandard housing. Many tables and charts.

256   ROWNTREE, B. SEEBOHM, and KENDALL, MAY. How the Labourer Lives, a Study of the Rural Labor Problem. London: Thomas Nelson & Sons, 1913. 342 pp.
      These case histories analyze spending and food consumption of families whose earnings are 12 to 15 shillings per week. The women do occasional agricultural work, laundry, or sewing, but their main contribution to family maintenance is thrifty housekeeping.

257   ROYAL PHOTOGRAPHIC SOCIETY. Directory of British Photographic Collections. Compiled by John Wall. London: Heinemann, 1977.
      Entry information includes: owner, location, and title of collection; custodian, dates covered, history, photographer(s), subjects, number of photographs, aids (such as indexes or catalogues), access, availability of copies, and charges. Not all of these items apply to every entry, but in general the information seems quite complete. Main entries are arranged under broad subject headings, of which the geographical seemed most fruitful, since pictures of work often are included in local history collections. There are indexes by subject, owner, location, title, and photographer.

258   ROYDEN, A. MAUDE, ed. Downward Paths. London: G. Bell & Sons, 1916. 200 pp.
      How do women become prostitutes? This study examines case histories. A chapter deals with the low wages and poor working conditions of women's occupations as contributing factors. Appendixes analyze home backgrounds and previous occupations of prostitutes. Bibliography.

259   SAMUELSON, JAMES. The Lament of the Sweated. London: P. S. King & Son, 1908. 68 pp.
      A barrister summarizes the findings of a House of Commons Select Committee report on sweated labor (1908) with vivid descriptions of the working and living conditions of the workers. Dramatic contrast is provided by opening the book with a description of a great ball. He appeals to the public to put pressure on members of Parliament to support anti-sweating legislation. Appendixes include a wages table and an abstract of a Sweated Industries bill.

260   SCHMIECHEN, JAMES A. "State Reform and the Local Economy." Economic History Review, 2d ser. 28 (1975):413-28.
      State intervention through protective legislation had the unplanned effect of reversing the trend toward

centralization of production. Small, frequently moved workshops or outwork avoided inspection and legal control. Therefore "in the eyes of the workers, state 'reform' was a factor which produced social disorganization." The workers, particularly women, became more aware of the usefulness of political action. Schmiechen bases his interpretation on study of the Islington, South Kensington, Marylebone, and Poplar vestries in London.

261 SCHREINER, OLIVE. Woman and Labour. London: T. Fisher Unwin, 1911. 283 pp.
     This feminist classic demands for women a share of "honoured and socially useful human toil." Schreiner argues that women's evolution has been stunted by their parasitism. She envisions the advantages for both sexes of a world in which women work as men do, and men share the humane concerns of women.

262 SCOTLAND. BOARD OF AGRICULTURE. Report on Home Industries in the Highlands and Islands, by W. R. Scott. Edinburgh: HMSO, 1914 (Cd.7564)
     The industries surveyed include spinning and weaving, lace making, wicker work, and basket making. Detailed suggestions include reducing the time between work and payment, and improving the design of hand-crafted items. Home industry is awarded an educational value in teaching work habits to rural young people.

263 SCOTTISH COUNCIL FOR WOMEN'S TRADES. Report of the National Conference on Sweated Industries. Glasgow: The Council, 1907. 95 pp.
     Peter Fyfe reported on female home-workers in Glasgow; Ramsay Macdonald discussed licensing proposals for home-workers; Clementina Black gave a paper on the health of homeworkers and the problem of contagious diseases.

263a SCOTTISH COUNCIL FOR WOMEN'S TRADES AND UNION FOR THE ABOLITION OF SWEATING. Handbook. Exhibition of Sweated Industries, Glasgow, 5-29 March 1913. Glasgow, 1913. 76 pp.
     Among the exhibits were items made by sweated labor, with statistics on time, rates, and deductions. A housing exhibit compared a Glasgow slum house with a model worker's house. Another displayed food items canned in a Scottish Council for Women's Trades factory under model conditions. An advertisement offers "Miss Irwin's Bottled Rasps" picked and canned at her fruit farm in Perthshire by women on a holiday from sweated labor.

264 SHAW, GEORGE BERNARD. Women as Councillors. Fabian Tract no. 93. London: Fabian Society, 1900. 4 pp.

Shaw argues that women are needed on county and borough councils to represent the needs of women (his example is public lavatories) and to inject a female voice into the planning for council housing.

265   SHAXBY, M.   "The Workers' Educational Association." *Women's Trades Union Review*, no. 78 (July 1910):12-18.
      The WEA existed to establish relations between workers and university, forming "links to connect up the demand with the supply." Summer programs were offered at universities, and other classes at the workplace or in neighbor-·hoods. Women's special problems in getting to class are acknowledged.

266   SILVERSTONE, ROSALIE.   "Office Work for Women: an Historical Review." *Business History* 18 (1976):98-110.
      ·Women entering clerical work were handicapped by inadequate education, especially in mathematics. Women from middle-class backgrounds, receiving very low wages, frequently spent so much of their money on respectable clothes that they ate poorly.

267   SMITH, ELLEN.   *Wage-Earning Women and Their Dependents*. London: Fabian Society, 1915. 36 pp.
      An investigation of 5,325 women workers found that fifteen percent were not self-supporting, thirty-three percent were, and fifty-one percent contributed to the support of others.

268   SOCIETY FOR THE STUDY OF LABOUR HISTORY. *Bulletin* 1 (1960-).
      The annual bibliographies of published material in the field of labor history are comprehensive. "Notes on sources" and annual classified lists of archive depositories provide information on primary source material.

269   SOLDON, NORBERT C.   *Women in British Trade Unions, 1874-1976*. Dublin: Gill & Macmillan, 1978. 226 pp.
      The years 1886-1914 are discussed in Chapter 2, "League into Union: the era of Lady Dilke 1886-1903," and Chapter 3 "Mary [Macarthur] and Margaret [Bondfield] 1903-1914." The account of the Women's Trade Union League, though brief, gives special attention to textile workers including Irish linen weavers, and discusses the problems of organizing women workers. The Sweated Industries Exhibition, the history of the Trade Boards Act, the organization of the Cradley Heath chainmakers, and the Bermondsey strike of 1911 are described. The author analyses the struggle between adult suffragists (who wanted to eliminate property qualifications for all voters) and woman suffragists (who were willing to accept the existing requirements, thereby extending the vote to women of the propertied class only),

and the changing attitudes of the Women's Social and Political Union toward working women. Although other studies
deal more extensively with specific aspects, this is a good
comprehensive history. Bibliography.

270 SPENCER, EDWARD. "Women and the Handicrafts." Englishwoman
12 (October-December 1911):56-67.
Because they have never been in the trade unions, women
handicraft workers have an opportunity to develop a different kind of organization for their trades. With the aim of
maintaining high standards of quality, Spencer proposes
establishment of a system including apprenticeship, appor-
tionment of work, and some form of price-fixing. An Arts
and Crafts Movement philosophy and belief in the moral
superiority of women are evident in this article. (An
announcement of a crafts exhibition sponsored by the journal is inserted opposite the first page of the essay.)

271 SQUIRE, ROSE. Thirty Years in the Public Service, an Industrial Retrospect. London: Nisbet & Co., 1927. 238 pp.
Rose Squire was a factory inspector from 1895 until her
retirement in 1926. Her work is the subject of this memoir,
with chapters on factory sanitation, industrial disease,
hours of work, wages, the Truck Act, and the 1906-07 Poor
Law investigation in which she participated. Her observations are vivid and detailed; like Adelaide Anderson (see
entry 5), she conveys a sense of adventure as well as sym-
pathy with the workers and a conviction of accomplishment.

272 STEARNS, PETER. Lives of Labour. London: Croom, Helm, 1975.
424 pp.
The apparent broadening of opportunities for working-
class women in the late nineteenth century heightened the
expectations of unmarried women. In fact, Stearns says,
after marriage they found themselves shut out of jobs, less
in control of household finances than formerly, and increasingly cut off as men developed leisure interests in pubs
and sports that excluded women. This provocative book also
suggests that further study of the relationship between
working-class and middle-class women is needed.

273 STEWART, MARGARET, and HUNTER, L. The Needle is Threaded:
the History of an Industry. Southampton: Heinemann, 1964.
241 pp.
Commissioned by the National Union of Tailors and Garment
Workers, this is a detailed history of the development of
tailors' organization, from the guilds to 1960. The reaction of men to women in this industry seems to have been
reasonably favorable: recognizing that unorganized women
presented a threat to wage levels and working conditions,
they included them in the union. There is no bibliography,

but an "Author's Note" mentions the chief sources; footnotes, when given, are not precise citations.

274 STRACHEY, RAY. <u>The Cause, a Short History of the Women's
     Movement in Great Britain</u>. London: G. Bell & Sons, 1928.
     Reprint, with new preface by Barbara Strachey. London:
     Virago, 1978. 429 pp.
         This thorough, clear history of the women's movement was
     written by an active participant, Ray Strachey. A friend
     of Millicent Fawcett, she was editor of the <u>Common Cause</u>
     and founder of the Women's Employment Federation. Her book
     provides a particularly strong account of the role of middle-
     class and upper-class women, with material on women's entry
     into the professions and their participation in trade unions
     and philanthropic activities. She pinpoints 1911 as the
     year when feminists and women labor leaders diverged, the
     latter feeling greater strength in their alliance with
     labor men.
         Barbara Strachey's preface to the 1978 reprint supplies
     a biography of the author.

275 _____. <u>Millicent Garrett Fawcett</u>. London: John Murray,
     1931. 380 pp.
         A friend and colleague writes an admiring biography of
     the tenacious leader of the nonmilitant suffragists. (<u>See</u>
     entry 87.)

276 SWANWICK, HELEN M. <u>I Have Been Young</u>. London: Victor
     Gollancz, 1935. 512 pp.
         Helen Swanwick was active in the National Union for
     Women's Suffrage and a friend of Millicent Fawcett. She
     edited the <u>Common Cause</u>, the NUWS weekly, from its founding
     in 1909 until 1912, and was a free-lance journalist for the
     <u>Manchester Guardian</u> and others. Her autobiography is well
     written and contains interesting material about the people
     she knew and about her own activities.

277 SYMONDS, E. M. [George Paston]. <u>The Career of Candida</u>.
     London: Chapman & Hall, 1896. 289 pp.
         Candida, the novel's central character, whose father
     brought her up like a boy, becomes a teacher of gymnastics.
     The book's bitter conclusion leaves her the sole support of
     her crippled husband and child.

278 THOMPSON, PAUL, AND HARKELL, GINA. <u>The Edwardians in Photo-
     graphs</u>. New York: Holmes & Meier, 1979. 128 pp.
         Photographs of Edwardians of all social classes at work
     and play.

279 TUCKWELL, GERTRUDE M. "The Industrial Position of Women."
     <u>Independent Review</u>, August 1904, pp. 365-76.

Tuckwell, a leader of the trade union movement, stresses the importance of labor organization for women; the existence of a large unorganized labor force is a threat to all workers.

280   _____. Women in Industry, From Seven Points of View. London: Duckworth & Co., 1908. 217 pp.
The seven public lectures published here are: "The Regulation of Women's Work," by Gertrude Tuckwell; "The Minimum Wage," by Constance Smith; "Trade Unionism," by Mary Macarthur; "Infantile Mortality," by May Tennant; "Child Employment and Juvenile Delinquency," by Nettie Adler; "Factory and Workshop Law," by Adelaide Anderson; and "Legislative Proposals," by Clementina Black. Black supports regulation by law as the only way to enable employers to risk changes in working conditions.

281   TWINING, LOUISA. "Official Work of Women." Englishwoman's Review 30 (1899):81-85.
_____. "Women as Official Inspectors." Nineteenth Century, March 1894, pp. 489-94.
_____. "Women as Public Servants." Nineteenth Century, December 1890, pp. 950-58.
Twining advocates increased use of women as official inspectors, on boards of guardians, and on management committees of hospitals, lunatic asylums, prisons, and penitentiaries. Women who are trained in medicine are particularly qualified for work with hospitals and infirmaries, and nurses will find it easier to confer with them.

282   VAN BLARCOM, CAROLYN CONANT. The Midwife in England: Being a Study in England of the Working of the English Midwives Act of 1902. Philadelphia: William F. Fell Co., 1913. 141 pp.
The intention of this report is to encourage legislation in the United States requiring training and licensing of midwives.

283   VICINUS, MARTHA. The Industrial Muse: a Study of Nineteenth-Century British Working-Class Literature. London: Croom Helm; New York: Harper & Row, 1974. 357 pp.
A study of such working-class means of expression as dialect literature, poetry, and music-hall performances, for which the author has gathered an extraordinary amount of material. Vicinus points out that as these forms became generally accepted and widely disseminated they lost much of their originality and specificity. Thorough bibliography and footnotes.

284   VYNNE, NORA, and BLACKBURN, HELEN. Women Under the Factory Acts. London: Williams & Norgate, 1903. 205 pp.
Restating in simple language the Factory Acts of 1901 as they affect the employer and the employee, the authors

also criticize those aspects of the law that seem to them
unfair or unreasonable. They object to such provisions as
may discriminate unfairly against the hiring of women for
certain jobs; to elements that seem to discourage good employers from being generous, or to discriminate against
small businesses; and to provisions they consider to inhibit
the right of individuals to work as much as they want to.
They advocate strict adherence to the law followed by peti-
tion to Parliament if the effect is unfair.

285   WALKOWITZ, JUDITH. Prostitution and Victorian Society.
      Cambridge: Cambridge University Press, 1980. 347 pp.
          Walkowitz finds that most women who became prostitutes
      entered the life on a casual basis to satisfy a temporary
      need for money, and that by identifying and isolating them,
      legislation made it more difficult for them to escape once
      they had begun. Her study includes legislation beginning
      with the Contagious Diseases Acts, the reform movements,
      and feminist political activity. Before World War I, with
      no medication to cure venereal disease, doctors agreed with
      the view of the social purity movement that chastity was
      the only solution. Feminists (who learned much about mili-
      tancy from this campaign) blamed the double standard.
      Walkowitz supports her argument with case studies of women
      in Plymouth and Southampton. Bibliography.

286   WALTON, RONALD G. Women in Social Work. London and Boston:
      Routledge & Kegan Paul, 1975. 308 pp.
          The author traces the development of social work from
      1860 to 1971, with particular attention to the contribu-
      tions of women and to the growth of professional training
      and standards.

287   WARBURTON, WILLIAM HENRY. History of Trade Union Organization
      in the North Staffordshire Potteries. London: George
      Allen & Unwin, 1931. 288 pp.
          Warburton states strongly that the potters made a mis-
      take in failing to include women as equal members in the
      trade unions from the start. Employers hired women at
      lower wages as mechanization took place (although it was
      slower and less complete in this industry than in most).
      Men never allowed women to pass the apprentice stage. This
      general history of organization in the potteries gives few
      hints on sources after 1870 except newspapers and journals,
      but it would be interesting to know more about women's
      role in the industry. Bibliography.

288   WEBB, BEATRICE POTTER. "East London Labour." Nineteenth
      Century, August 1888, pp. 161-83.
          In a general report on the structure of the tailoring
      trade, the author compares trade in East London with that
      in the West End.

289   _____. <u>How Best to Do Away With the Sweating System</u>. Paper read at the 24th annual Congress of Co-operative Societies, Rochdale, June 1892. Manchester, n.d. 16 pp.
     The best way to abolish home-work is by extending the Factory Acts to regulate it. Cooperators are urged to bring pressure on Parliament to achieve this.

290   _____. "The Pages of a Work Girl's Diary." <u>Nineteenth Century</u>, September 1888, pp. 301-14.
     As part of an investigation, the author worked as a trouser finisher in an East London tailoring establishment. She found the mistress treated her fairly, and her fellow workers were kind.

291   _____. <u>The Wages of Men and Women: Should They Be Equal?</u> London: Fabian Society, 1919. 79 pp.
     This publication endorses a national minimum wage, standard occupational rates, provision of child care, a minimum working age of eighteen for workers except in learning situations, and no exclusion from any job on account of sex.

292   WEBB, CATHERINE. "An Unpopular Industry." <u>Nineteenth Century</u> 43 (January-June 1903):989-1001.
     The Women's Industrial Council sponsored a survey about domestic service and why people didn't like it as an occupation. Most respondents were mistresses (forty-four) and people who trained servants (twenty-five), with some members of the Women's Co-operative Guild, and only ten servants. Low social status and lack of freedom emerge as the main reasons for dislike of the occupation, but it must be remembered that these are mainly the opinions of employers.

293   WEBB, SIDNEY. "The Alleged Differences of the Wages Paid to Men and Women for Similar Work." <u>Economic Journal</u> 1 (1891): 635-62.
     Comparing men's and women's wages in the United States and England in manual, "routine mental" (i.e., post office), professional, and intellectual work, Webb finds that disparities were often accounted for by differences in duties, and were reduced when both men and women were better suited to their jobs. Among his recommendations to improve women's wages: "greater public influence of women," higher physical standards (women should eat more), technical training, better education, and greater independence. For another viewpoint, see Millicent Garrett Fawcett, "Mr. Sidney Webb's Article on Women's Wages," entry 85.

294   WEBB, SIDNEY, and WEBB, BEATRICE POTTER. <u>The Letters of Sidney and Beatrice Webb</u>. 3 vols. Edited by Norman MacKenzie. Cambridge: Cambridge University Press, 1978.

These selected letters were written before and during
this famous marriage, between 1873 and 1947. Each volume
has an index and a list of recipients.
For further information, see Kitty Muggeridge and Ruth
Adam, Beatrice Webb: a Life, entry 212.

295   WERNER, A. "The Fish Curing Industry." Englishwoman's Review,
       no. 263 (1904), pp. 232-35.
       Contradicting the findings in Oliver's Dangerous Trades
       (see entry 227), Werner argues that overtime work in the
       fish curing industry is compensated by short hours (or none)
       in the slack season. Fresh fish must be dealt with imme-
       diately, and inclusion of this industry under the Factory
       Acts will mean that the work will be given to men. This
       author describes the work as reasonably healthy because it
       is performed outdoors, and well paid.

296   WILLOUGHBY DE BROKE, MARIE. "The Pros and Cons of Domestic
       Service." National Review 60 (1912):452-60.
       Having assisted in a Women's Industrial Council investi-
       gation of domestic service, Lady Willoughby de Broke sug-
       gests that many problems could be avoided if employers took
       more sympathetic interest in their servants. A protective
       mistress, she opposes the idea of servants living in
       hostels.

297   WILSON, MONA. Our Industrial Laws: Working Women in Facto-
       ries, Workshops, Shops and Laundries, and How to Help Them.
       Edited and with a preface by Mrs. H. J. Tennant. Issued
       by the Industrial Law Committee. London: Duckworth & Co.,
       1899. 79 pp.
       An outline of laws affecting women workers, this was
       prepared to assist social workers in spotting and acting
       on violations.

298   The Woman Worker. Journal of the Federation of Women Workers.
       Edited by Mary Macarthur. 1907-10, 1916-21.
       In addition to news of the Women's Trade Union League
       and the Women's Labour League, this journal includes sto-
       ries and poems, news of legislation and the suffrage move-
       ment, and biographies of notable women.

299   "Women in Industry." New Statesmen 2(46) (February 21, 1914)
       special supplement.
       The essays, presented by the Fabian Women's Group, in-
       clude: Introduction, by Mrs. Sidney Webb; "Women's Wages,"
       by Mrs. F. W. Hubback; "Women in Trade Unionism," by B. L.
       Hutchins; "The Legal Minimum Wage at Work," by J. J. Mallon;
       and "A Policy for Women Workers," by Mrs. Pember Reeves and
       Mrs. C. M. Wilson. Technical training, political equality,
       a minimum wage, and child care provisions are among the
       reforms recommended. Bibliography.

300   "Women in Libraries." Englishwoman's Review 30 (1899):240-45.
        Women are described as good library workers, content
        with salaries too low to satisfy men. A list of libraries
        with women librarians or assistant librarians is included.

301   Women in Rebellion--1900: Two Views on Class, Socialism and
        Liberation. Square One Pamphlet no. 6. Leeds: Independ-
        ent Labour Party Square One Publications, 1973.
        Two polemical pamphlets, including "Working Women and
        the Suffrage" by Mrs. Wibaut, and "Woman's Freedom" by
        Lily Gair Wilkinson, from the International Labour Party
        archives are uninformatively introduced by Suzie Fleming.
        Wibaut's thesis is that the housewife performs unpaid labor
        for her husband's capitalist employer by doing work her
        husband would otherwise have to do himself or pay someone
        to do. Wilkinson argues for a new classless society in
        preference to reformation of the suffrage. The value of
        presenting these two arguments would have been much en-
        hanced by the presence of biographical information and a
        historical setting.

302   WOMEN'S CO-OPERATIVE GUILD. A Minimum Wage Scale for Co-
        operative Women and Girl Employees. Manchester: Co-
        operative Wholesale Society's Printing Works, 1910. 12 pp.
        This statement supports a petition signed by 13,337
        members of the Guild for the adoption of a minimum wage
        scale for women cooperative employees. "We desire to set
        the pace in civilizing the conditions of labour. . . ."

303   _____. Report of Investigations into the Conditions of Women's
        Work. London: Women's Co-operative Guild, 1896. 16 pp.
        Seeing a need for an expression of the views of working
        women on the Factory Act, how far it was effective, and
        what further legislation was needed, the Guild presented
        papers to its branches and gathered the opinions of the
        members on such subjects as reduction of hours of work,
        abolition of home-work, and factory inspection.

304   _____. Women Employees in Co-operative Stores and Factories.
        Oxford: Women's Co-operative Guild, 1910.
        This reports on efforts of the Guild to persuade women
        to join the Amalgamated Union of Co-operative Employees and
        to achieve a minimum wage in cooperative factories.

305   WOMEN'S INDUSTRIAL COUNCIL. Annual Reports. 1st through 20th,
        1894-95/1913-14.
        The Council conducted investigations and published re-
        ports on industries in which women were employed; provided
        help to individual women workers in response to complaints;
        provided a library and picture-lending service for working
        girls' clubs; and maintained a lecture service. The Council

organized and ran the Association of Trained Charladies, a
training and employment center. Annual reports (the British Museum has the eighth through the fourteenth, 1901-08)
include lists of names of council and committee members,
subscription and donation lists, and reports of the councils and committees.

306   . The Case For and Against a Legal Minimum Wage for
Sweated Workers. London: Women's Industrial Council,
1909. 24 pp.
    "Sweated conditions are part of the disorganization
which exists on the margins of industry," a fact that makes
enforcement of legislation difficult.

307   . Home Industries of Women in London, 1906. Interim
Report of an Inquiry by the Investigation Committee of the
Women's Industrial Council. London: Women's Industrial
Council, 1908. 169 pp.
    Clementina Black's "Tabulated Cases" of forty-four
women engaged in home-work in a variety of trades, their
hours, earnings, and living conditions, provide a vivid
picture of the home-worker's life in London. Margaret
Macdonald wrote sections on British law and on American
legislation. Information on conditions in Germany,
Australia, and New Zealand is included.

308   . "Report of the National Conference on the Unemployment
of Women Dependent on Their Own Earnings, Held in the Council Chamber of the Guildhall, London, E.C., on Tuesday,
October 15th, 1907." Women's Industrial News, December
1907, pp. 669-705.
    The conference discussed slack-season unemployment;
training women to take up other trades; and methods of
dealing with the unemployment of husbands, which increased
their wives' problems. A memorandum recommending methods
of alleviating unemployment was sent from the conference to
the Local Government Board. (In June 1908 another meeting
was reported, which was held to protest the lack of response
from the Local Government Board.)

309   . Technical Education for Girls in England and Elsewhere.
London: Women's Industrial Council, 1897. 12 pp.
    In Europe, girls receive training in domestic science
and other technical skills. In England only the "3 R's,
a little sewing, perhaps a little cooking and laundry work."

310   . Technical Education for Women and Girls at Home and
Abroad. London: Women's Industrial Council, 1905. 64 pp.
    Describing existing training programs in London, the
report praises the Waistcoat Making School at the Borough
Polytechnic, and says that more such programs are needed.

It also recommends scholarships and full day programs to include general education as well as skills training.

311   . Women's Wages in England in the Nineteenth Century. London: Women's Industrial Council, 1906. 11 pp.
    Commenting on the difficulty of obtaining retrospective information on wages, the pamphlet nevertheless makes careful comparisons. It recommends reduction of child labor to make more jobs for women, and more training to make women better able to compete; it voices a fear of competition from the "yellow races."

312   Women's Industrial News, n.s. 1-55, September 1897-October 1911.
    This valuable contemporary source includes "Industrial Notes" on problems of women workers (for example, home-workers making coronation flags); reports of investigations, conferences, and committees.

313   WOMEN'S INSTITUTE, LONDON. The Women's Institute. London: The Institute, 1897. 13 pp.
    Founded "on strictly non-party lines," the Women's Institute was a center of information and a meeting place for men and women engaged in professional work. The program included lectures, instruction in business skills, music, and recreational activities; the reference library specialized in subjects concerning women.

314   WOMEN'S TRADE UNION ASSOCIATION. How Women Work, Being Extracts from Evidence Given Before Group C of the Labour Commission in Regard to Women Working in the Ropemaking and Other Trades in London. London: The Association, n.d. 11 pp.
    As secretary of the Women's Ropemakers' Union, Annie Hicks testified on excessive hours worked and on work-related injuries in support of the need for women factory inspectors.

315   The Women's Trades Union Review. Quarterly. 1891-1919.
    The official journal of the Women's Trade Union League includes reports of its meetings; reports on unions, meetings, and strikes; on factory legislation; on prosecutions under the Factory Acts; and on Parliamentary actions and discussions pertaining to women's work.

316   WOODHAM-SMITH, CECIL. Florence Nightingale, 1820-1910. London: Constable & Co., 1950. 615 pp.
    Although most of Nightingale's work was done before the 1890s, she was still a formidable opponent when the British Nurses' Association and the Hospitals' Association proposed to standardize the qualifications for trained nurses by establishing a registry of nurses that based admission on

examination. Her opposition was based on her belief that character training was as important for nurses as technical skill. She was not a supporter of opening new fields of work to women, or of women's suffrage. The biography portrays a difficult, exasperating, powerful woman, capable of enormous feats of statistical research and synthesis, as well as political persuasion, who worked for over half a century from an invalid's seclusion.

317 Work and Leisure, a Magazine Devoted to the Interests of Women, London, 1875-93.
     This magazine for gentlewomen carries suggestions for money-making crafts, cheap vacations, and thrifty housekeeping; warning articles by women who have been defrauded; and classified advertisements placed by distressed gentlewomen. Little of the material is truly practical, and the general effect is pathetic.

318 ZIMMERN, ALICE. "Ladies' Dwellings." Contemporary Review 77 (1900):96-104.
     The author describes several experiments in housing for educated working women that supply comfortable living space, privacy, and shared cooking and dining facilities at reasonable cost.

319 _____. Unpaid Professions for Women. London: Guardian Office, 1906. 86 pp.
     Directed at middle-class and upper-class women, this essay that originally appeared in the Guardian suggests as possible vocations: charity work, settlement work, recreation, service to working women, work among young servants, educational administration, council and guardian activities, and church work. It encourages training and a professional attitude toward volunteer work. An appendix lists organizations and training centers in London.

Women's Work in America

320 ABBOTT, EDITH. "Employment of Women in Industries: Cigar Making, Its History and Present Tendencies." Journal of Political Economy 15 (1907):1-25.
Early Connecticut farmers' wives made cigars at home. When the industry moved into the factory, men displaced women; but immigration brought in skilled Bohemian and German women. Women's wages were lower than men's.

321 _____. "Industrial Employment of Women." Journal of Political Economy 14 (1906):461-502.
Reviewing the history of women's work in America since the seventeenth century, the author concludes that women have been an important factor in industry all along. It is the middle-class woman for whom financial independence is a new idea, not the working-class woman.

322 ABBOTT, FRANCES M. "Three Decades of College Women." Popular Science Monthly 65 (1904):350-59.
This analysis of the careers pursued by Vassar graduates of the classes 1867-96 finds that the greatest number of professionals were teachers. Few had entered science or medicine; the number in settlement work had increased; eight were farmers.

323 ABBOTT, GRACE. "The Midwife in Chicago." American Journal of Sociology 20 (March 1915):684-99.
Citing British precedent, Abbott argues for a system of training, examination, and registration for midwives in the United States. She points out that many immigrants employ midwives in preference to male doctors. (See entry 282.)

324 ADDAMS, JANE. Democracy and Social Ethics. New York: Macmillan, 1907. Reprint. Edited by Anne Firor Scott. Cambridge: Harvard University Press, 1964. 281 pp.
Addams demonstrates her awareness of the difficulties of the middle-class social worker in understanding and

responding to the needs of her clients. The relationship
of the middle-class working woman and her family is examined in "Filial Relations" (pp. 71-101). In "Household
Adjustment" (pp. 102-36) she discusses the domestic servant
and her relationship with her employer.

Scott provides an extensive introductory essay on
Addams's life and work.

325   . My Friend, Julia Lathrop. New York: Macmillan, 1935.
228 pp.
Julia Lathrop was a resident of Hull House, a member of
the Illinois State Board of Charities, and a fighter for
reform. Her particular interest was finding more humane
ways of caring for the mentally ill. In this memoir Jane
Addams concentrates on Lathrop's work before 1912.

326   . The Spirit of Youth and the City Streets. New York:
Macmillan, 1910. 162 pp.
This collection of essays concentrates on the needs of
young working people for education, art, music, and play,
and the harmful results of failure to provide these needs.

327   . Twenty Years at Hull House. New York: Macmillan,
1910. Reprint. New York: New American Library, n.d.
320 pp.
Addams's autobiography centers on her work at Hull House,
the struggle for legislation on child labor and hours of
work, and her views on various problems of society.

328 ALLAND, ALEXANDER. Jessie Tarbox Beals, First Woman News
Photographer. New York: Camera/Graphic Press, 1978.
92 pp. 95 plates.
Beals (1870-1942) began as a schoolteacher but became
interested in photography and established a studio in
Williamsburg, Massachusetts. She had a keen eye for business and a restless urge to travel. Her broad scope included portraits, architectural and scenic photography,
and photojournalism. She became nationally known when
she photographed the St. Louis World's Fair.

329 ALLOY, EVELYN. Working Women's Music: the Songs and Struggles
of Women in the Cotton Mills. Somerville, Mass.: New
England Free Press, 1976. 44 pp.
This collection of songs is accompanied by illustrations
and a brief explanatory text. The earliest songs were
written in 1810.

330 AMMER, CHRISTINE. Unsung: a History of Women in American
Music. Westport, Conn. and London: Greenwood Press, 1980.
317 pp.
Ammer surveys women's activities as soloists, members
and conductors of orchestras, composers, and teachers of

music. The period 1890–1914 was extremely active. This is
a necessary introduction to the subject, and includes biographical material on major figures; it should inspire further work.

331   ANDERSON, MARY. <u>Woman at Work: the Autobiography of Mary
      Anderson as Told to Mary N. Winslow</u>. Minneapolis: Uni-
      versity of Minnesota Press; London: Oxford University,
      1951. 266 pp.
          Mary Anderson, the trade union leader who became head
      of the Department of Labor's Women's Bureau, tells the
      story of her life from her Swedish childhood and immigra-
      tion to the United States at the age of sixteen, through
      her early work experience in domestic service and factory
      work, activity in the labor movement, and her government
      service.

331a ANTHONY, KATHARINE. <u>Mothers Who Must Earn</u>. West Side Studies,
      Russell Sage Foundation. New York: Survey Associates,
      1914. 223 pp.
          This report is based on an investigation of 370 working
      mothers who lived on the West Side in New York City. It
      is a rich source of information on living accommodations
      and neighborhoods, as well as occupations ranging from
      office cleaner to home laundress to news dealer.

332   ANTIN, MARY. <u>From Plotzk to Boston</u>. Boston: W. B. Clarke &
      Co., 1899. 80 pp. Reprint (microfilm). In <u>History of
      Women</u>, no. 3795. New Haven, Conn.: Research Publications,
      1975.
          _____. <u>The Promised Land</u>. Boston and New York: Houghton
      Mifflin, 1912. 373 pp.
          Mary Antin came from Russia to Boston with her family
      as a child. While her older brothers and sisters worked,
      she went to school and began writing. These two autobio-
      graphical books discuss her experience as an immigrant and
      the help and encouragement she received from teachers and
      editors.

332a ARTHUR AND ELIZABETH SCHLESINGER LIBRARY ON THE HISTORY OF
      WOMEN IN AMERICA. <u>The Manuscript Inventories and the Cata-
      logs of Manuscripts, Books, and Pictures, Arthur and
      Elizabeth Schlesinger Library on the History of Women in
      America, Radcliffe College, Cambridge, Massachusetts</u>.
      3 vols. Boston: G. K. Hall, 1973.
          This catalogue provides a guide to one of the major
      library collections on the history of American women. Al-
      though much retrospective material has been added since
      1973, the catalogue is an extremely useful guide to pub-
      lished works as well as to the Schlesingers' manuscript
      and picture collections.

333 ASHBAUGH, CAROLYN. Lucy Parsons, American Revolutionary.
     Chicago: C. H. Kerr, 1976. 288 pp.
         Lucy Parsons played an active role in the radical labor
     movement, especially in Chicago. Ashbaugh has gathered
     information not available elsewhere, but the book fails to
     distinguish between the significant and the trivial.

334 ATKINSON, LINDA. Mother Jones, the Most Dangerous Woman in
     America. New York: Crown, 1978. 246 pp.
         A biography of the labor organizer and strike leader
     that emphasizes her originality and courage. Based on
     secondary sources, it offers little insight into the char-
     acter of this extraordinary woman. See Dale Fetherling,
     Mother Jones, the Miners' Angel (entry 397) for a closer
     look at her role as a folk hero; and Mother Jones's auto-
     biography (entry 432), upon which both biographies depend.

335 AURAND, HAROLD W. "Diversifying the Economy of the Anthracite
     Regions, 1880-1900." Pennsylvania Magazine of History and
     Biography 94 (1970):54-61.
         As a measure of protection against the uneven employment
     of miners, anthracite towns in Pennsylvania tried to en-
     courage establishment of other industries such as silk mills
     and bakeries. Although they added little to the economy
     and paid low wages, these industries provided employment
     for the women of mining families.

336 AUSTIN, ANNE L. The Woolsey Sisters of New York: 1860-1900.
     Philadelphia: American Philosophical Society, 1971.
     189 pp.
         Four of the seven Woolsey sisters were hospital nurses
     in the Civil War; three continued in nursing after the war.
     Georgeanna was instrumental in the establishment of a nurs-
     ing school in New Haven, Connecticut. Abby was active in
     the New York State Charities Aid Association. Based on
     family papers and diaries, the book tells the story but
     offers little interpretation.

337 BAER, JUDITH A. The Chains of Protection: the Judicial
     Response to Women's Labor Legislation. Westport, Conn.
     and London: Greenwood Press, 1978. 238 pp.
         Baer examines the development of public policy on pro-
     tection of working women in the United States. She explains
     the assumptions behind protective legislation and the chain
     of judicial decisions through which protection became re-
     striction. She concludes that in present-day American
     society such special legislation can be justified only by
     insisting on the priority of women's domestic role. A well-
     documented, intelligent book with a useful bibliography.

338 BAKER, GLADYS L. "Women in the U.S. Department of Agriculture."
      Agricultural History 50 (1976):190-201.
           Women in the Department of Agriculture worked as clerks
      and seed packers, but also as librarians and as researchers.
      Their ranks and salaries varied with the attitude of the
      incumbent secretary. This article, which covers a century
      beginning in 1870, provokes interest in this area of scien-
      tific occupation.

339 BAKER, S. JOSEPHINE. "Schools for Midwives." American
      Journal of Obstetrics and the Diseases of Women and Children
      65 (1912):256-70.
           Comparing midwife training in the United States with
      that in several European countries, this country is shown
      to be far behind. Baker makes specific recommendations for
      legal control, education, and supervision of midwives.

339a BALLOU, PATRICIA K. Women, a Bibliography of Bibliographies.
      Boston: G. K. Hall, 1980. 155 pp.
           This selective annotated bibliography lists bibliogra-
      phies published between 1970 and 1979. The detailed sub-
      ject arrangement includes sections on specific occupations
      as well as on labor history and on individual countries.

339b BANKS, ELIZABETH L. The Autobiography of a "Newspaper Girl."
      New York: Dodd-Mead, 1902, 317 pp.
           Banks was an American journalist who worked both in
      London and in New York. She posed as a servant and as a
      flower girl to obtain material for free-lance articles.
      She tells her story with a journalist's flair for the
      dramatic.

340 BANKS, LOUIS ALBERT. White Slaves: or, the Oppression of the
      Worthy Poor. Boston: Lee & Shepard, 1893. Reprint
      (microfilm). In History of Women, no. 3813. New Haven,
      Conn.: Research Publications, 1975. 327 pp.
           The "white slaves" are women and children doing home-
      work in Boston; their living conditions, rents, and wages
      are described.

341 BANNER, LOIS. "The American Woman from 1900 to the First
      World War: A Profile." In Women's Lives: Perspectives on
      Progress and Change, edited by Virginia Lee Lussier and
      Joyce Jennings Walstedt, pp. 93-119. Newark: University
      of Delaware, 1977. Reprinted from The Underside of History:
      Other Readings, 2d ed., edited by Thomas R. Frazier. New
      York: Harcourt Brace Jovanovich, 1974.
           Banner summarizes clearly the social position and work
      of American women during this period and the effect on
      their lives of changing views of women's sexuality. She
      points out that questions about women raised during this
      time continued to be debated for years afterward.

342   BARNETT, IDA B. WELLS. <u>Crusade for Justice: The Autobiogra-</u><u>phy of Ida B. Wells</u>. Edited by Alfreda M. Duster. Chicago and London: University of Chicago Press, 1970. 434 pp.
        Ida Wells-Barnett was a teacher and journalist. As a public speaker she traveled widely in the United States and England campaigning against racism and lynching. She was a leader in the National Association of Colored Women. Her unfinished autobiography vigorously describes the life and work of a thorough political activist.

343   BARRETT, KATE WALLER. <u>Some Practical Suggestions on the Con-</u><u>duct of a Rescue Home</u>. Washington, D.C.: National Florence Crittenton Mission, 1903. Reprint. New York: Arno Press, 1974. 115 pp.
        Barrett's recommendations, based on her own experience in setting up rescue homes for unmarried mothers, emphasize neatness and cleanliness, participation in household work, a family atmosphere, and advice. She believes that mothers should be encouraged to keep their babies and helped to find work, preferrably in domestic service and in the country.

344   BARRINGER, EMILY DUNNING. <u>Bowery to Bellevue, the Story of</u><u>New York's First Woman Ambulance Surgeon</u>. New York: W. W. Norton, 1950. 262 pp.
        The first woman physician to be an intern in a major New York hospital tells the story of her two years (1903-04), replete with anecdotes. She rode the horse-drawn ambulances, performed emergency surgery, and worked on the wards despite the hostility of her fellow interns and residents. This is a vivid account of a pioneer's experience.

344a BARROWS, ISABEL C. "Ellen Johnson and the Sherborn Prison." <u>New England Magazine</u>, n.s. 21 (1899-1900):614-33.
        Sherborn Prison under Ellen Johnson's administration was considered a model prison for women. Barrows describes the institution and Johnson's system of reform, and provides a biography of Johnson.

345   BAXANDALL, ROSALYN; GORDON, LINDA; and REVERBY, SUSAN, comps. <u>America's Working Women</u>. New York: Random House, 1976. 408 pp.
        This collection of documents includes excerpts from personal accounts, government, union, and social agency reports, journal articles, and books. The brief selections are grouped by subject; each section is preceded by an editorial comment. Both documents and illustrations are well selected; the reader who wants more can follow the footnotes to the source of the excerpt.

346   BEARD, MARY RITTER. Woman's Work in Municipalities. New
       York and London: D. Appleton & Co., 1915. 344 pp.
          The idea that "municipal housekeeping"--work with the
       purpose of improving conditions of urban life--was a natu-
       ral extension of women's sphere became current in the early
       years of the twentieth century. Here Beard discusses women
       in social service, teaching, street-cleaning campaigns,
       public health, recreational programs, and other work, both
       salaried and voluntary.

347   BERKIN, CAROL RUTH. "Private Woman, Public Woman: The Con-
       tradictions of Charlotte Perkins Gilman." In Women of
       America, edited by Carol Ruth Berkin and Mary Beth Norton,
       pp. 150-76. Boston: Houghton Mifflin, 1979.
          Berkin explores Gilman's difficulties in accommodating
       both her private emotional needs and her determination to
       work for social reform. Gilman believed the two were mu-
       tually exclusive, and only late in her life was she pre-
       pared to risk a serious emotional commitment. Berkin's
       analysis is convincing and might be applied to other social
       reformers as well.

348   Bibliography of College, Social, University and Church Settle-
       ments. 5th ed. Compiled by Caroline Williamson Montgomery.
       Chicago: College Settlements Association, 1905. 147 pp.
          A "General Bibliography of Settlements" is followed by
       a directory arranged by state and city. Each entry includes
       a brief history and statement of purpose, names of head
       residents, and a bibliography of reports, articles, and
       other publications about the settlement.

349   BIGGS, MARY. "Neither Printer's Wife Nor Widow: American
       Women in Typesetting, 1830-1950." Library Quarterly 50
       (1980):431-52.
          Concentrating on women who worked as typesetters in
       printing offices where they had no family connections,
       Biggs studies how women learned the trade, how the male
       typesetters viewed women as competitors, and the relation-
       ship of women typesetters to unions.

350   BLAIR, KAREN J. The Clubwoman as Feminist: True Womanhood
       Redefined, 1868-1914. New York and London: Holmes &
       Meier, 1980. 199 pp.
          Women's clubs, with their origins in literary groups,
       organizations of professional women, and service organiza-
       tions, helped to extend the concept of women's sphere into
       the public arena through social reform activities that they
       described as "municipal housekeeping." Although the clubs
       were generally conservative and often racist and nativist
       in outlook, they enabled women to gain confidence and to
       be active outside the home. They did not play a strong

role on behalf of working women or in the suffrage campaign.
Bibliography.

350a BLANC, MARIE THERESE. The Condition of Woman in the United
      States: a Traveller's Notes. Translated by Abby Langdon
      Alger. Boston: Roberts Brothers, 1895. 285 pp.
          Madame Blanc presents a Frenchwoman's observations on
      American women. She discusses women's clubs, colleges,
      settlements, and industrial schools, and describes the
      Chicago World's Fair. She compares the characteristics
      of women's activities in various major cities. Discussing
      prison conditions for women, she gives particular attention
      to Sherborn Prison, which, under the administration of Ellen
      Johnson, was considered a model.

351   BLISS, H. L. "Eccentric Official Statistics." American
      Journal of Sociology 3 (1897-98):355-77.
          Bliss criticizes Commissioner of Labor Carroll Wright's
      interpretation (see entry 548) of the statistics on employ-
      ment of women and children compiled in the Eleventh Census.
      Wright found that women were not "crowding upon men" in the
      labor market. Bliss finds flaws in Wright's method of com-
      paring these with earlier census returns and his failure to
      consider women sales clerks.

352   BLUMBERG, DOROTHY ROSE. Florence Kelley: the Making of Social
      Pioneer. New York: Augustus M. Kelley, 1966. 194 pp.
          As Chief Factory Inspector for the State of Illinois
      and secretary and inspector for the Consumers' League,
      Florence Kelley carried out her efforts to improve working
      conditions of women and children in industry. Blumberg dis-
      cusses her work, her family life, and her long acquaintance
      with Friedrich Engels.

353   BOONE, GLADYS. The Women's Trade Union Leagues in Great
      Britain and the United States of America. Columbia Uni-
      versity Studies in the Social Sciences, 489. New York:
      Columbia University Press, 1942. Reprint. New York:
      AMS Press, 1968. 283 pp.
          This compact account of the beginnings of the United
      States League, with a background section on Britain, is
      frequently cited as a source.

353a BOQUIST, CONSTANCE, and HAASE, JEANNETTE V. An Historical
      Review of Women in Dentistry: an Annotated Bibliography.
      Rockville, Md.: Office of Health Resources Opportunity;
      Cambridge: Radcliffe College, 1977. Available from EDRS:
      ED 148 223.
          This bibliography contains 263 citations and 162 abstracts
      of articles in medical and dental journals. It includes
      material about women in dentistry in the United States,
      Great Britain, and Europe during the years 1865-1977.

354 BRANCA, PATRICIA. "A New Perspective on Women's Work: a
Comparative Typology." Journal of Social History 9 (1975):
129-53.
Branca believes that scholars have not properly identi-
fied trends and attitudes as they have studied women's
work. After 1890, factory work became less important and
clerical work more so. In addition, historians must
include the study of informal work situations such as independent small businesses, dressmaking, and other services.
Women, she argues, prefer work that involves personal
relationships.

355 BRECKINRIDGE, SOPHONISBA P. Women in the Twentieth Century.
New York: McGraw-Hill, 1933. 364 pp. Index.
Women's employment, women's clubs and their activities,
and women's political activities from the 1890s until 1932
are surveyed in this compendium.

356 BRISLEY, MELISSA ANN. "Cornelia Marvin Pierce: Pioneer in
Library Extension." Library Quarterly 38 (1968):125-53.
Pierce brought library service to remote areas of
Wisconsin and Oregon through the introduction of county
libraries and books-by-mail service. As State Librarian
of Oregon she organized a vigorous legislative reference
service. The author finds her career an example of an
active and imaginative professional life in the Progressive
period.

357 BROWN, CHARLES B. "A Woman's Odyssey: the War Correspondence
of Anna Benjamin." Journalism Quarterly 46 (1969):522-30.
Anna Benjamin went to Cuba in 1898 to cover the Spanish-
American war. In 1899 she travelled in and reported from
the Philippines. This brief biography is based chiefly on
her articles in Leslies' and the New York Tribune.

358 BROWN, HARRIET CONNER. Grandmother Brown's Hundred Years,
1827-1927. Boston: Little, Brown, 1929. 369 pp.
Maria Foster Brown raised a large family in Ohio and
Iowa. Her daughter-in-law, a journalist, transcribed her
reminiscences, which are an intimate account of housekeeping
and parenting.

359 BRUNHES, MME. JEAN. L'Exemple des Americaines. Paris:
Ligue Sociale D'Archeteurs, 1903. 32 pp.
Twelve years after the founding of the Consumers' League
in New York, "the dawn of the movement," a French admirer
describes its beginnings and its activities.

360 BULLARD, ARTHUR [Albert Edwards]. Comrade Yetta. New York:
Macmillan, 1913. 448 pp.

This novel is about a Jewish girl on New York's Lower
East Side who works in a vest-making sweatshop, becomes
active in the trade-union movement in association with the
Women's Trade Union League, and learns to be an accomplished
newspaper writer. It is enriched with much historical
detail.

361   BULLOUGH, VERN, and BULLOUGH, BONNIE. The Care of the Sick:
       the Emergence of Modern Nursing. New York: Prodist, 1978.
       311 pp.
       A history of nursing with emphasis on the United States
       and Britain, this traces the development of training schools
       professional organizations, and public health nursing. The
       bibliography, though extensive, is not reliable.

362   BUTLER, ELIZABETH BEARDSLEY. Saleswomen in Mercantile Stores,
       Baltimore, 1909. New York: Charities Publication Commit-
       tee, 1912. 217 pp.
       At the request of the Consumers' League of Maryland, the
       Russell Sage Foundation sent Butler to investigate working
       conditions in Baltimore stores. The report describes seat-
       ing, lunch and rest accommodations, hours and wages, the
       problem of seasonal work, and the background of the sales-
       women. A final chapter discusses some pioneer programs in
       other cities for training saleswomen, arguing that trained
       women would be better able to compete and to demand living
       wages (which most Baltimore saleswomen were not receiving).
       A lucid, careful study.

363   _____. Women and the Trades, Pittsburgh, 1907-1908. New York:
       Charities Publication Committee, 1909. 440 pp.
       The Russell Sage Foundation sponsored this study of
       women employed in Pittsburgh factories, clothing trades,
       telephone and telegraph offices, and stores. Detailed in-
       formation about the industries includes wages, hours, con-
       ditions of work, hazards, training availability. Informatio
       about living conditions and recreation is also included.
       Problems include lack of opportunity for skilled work,
       exclusion from unions, inadequate pay; an obstacle to
       improvement is the women's own view of their work as
       temporary.

364   BYINGTON, MARGARET F. Homestead, the Households of a Mill
       Town. New York: Charities, 1910. Reprint. New York:
       Arno, 1969. 292 pp.
       The Homestead study, part of the Pittsburgh survey spon-
       sored by the Russell Sage Foundation, analyzes data from
       ninety households. Since the steel mills employed only
       men, few women were wage-earners. Most wives managed the
       family finances, and some took lodgers. Detailed informa-
       tion is given on housekeeping, budgets, and living condition

365 CAMPBELL, HELEN. Women Wage-Earners: Their Past, Their
     Present, and Their Future. Boston: Roberts Brothers,
     1893. 313 pp.
        After tracing the history of women factory workers,
     Campbell discusses problems of union organization, working
     conditions and wages in Eastern and Western states, and
     dangers and abuses to working women. She compares condi-
     tions in the United States with those in England, France,
     and Germany. Campbell recommends protective legislation,
     equal pay for equal work, and profit-sharing.

366 CARLSON, WILLIAM H. "Ida Angeline Kidder: Pioneer Western
     Land-Grant Librarian." College and Research Libraries
     29 (1968):217-23.
        Kidder became librarian of Oregon State Agricultural
     College in 1908 at the age of fifty-three, and remained
     in that position until her death in 1920.

367 CHENERY, WILLIAM L. Industry and Human Welfare. New York:
     Macmillan, 1922. 166 pp.
        Chenery, Industrial Editor of the Survey, discusses the
     effects (good and bad) of industry on workers in the United
     States. He points out that women have always worked, and
     factory work gave them some economic independence. He be-
     lieves state regulation of women's work is necessary because
     they seem unable to obtain decent conditions themselves.
     He favors elimination of hazardous work conditions rather
     than prohibition of employment of women, and advocates un-
     employment insurance, which would also encourage manufac-
     turers to stabilize production. Finally, he observes that
     "factories were built to increase human welfare" and urges
     more equitable distribution of wealth and shorter hours to
     provide more time for recreation.

368 COMSTOCK, SARAH. "The Lady and the Land: Some Scientific
     and Successful Women Farmers of America." Colliers,
     September 3, 1910, pp. 20-21, 24, 26-27.
        This illustrated article tells success stories of women
     farmers across the United States. Many of them seem to
     have come to farming as a refuge from the professions.

369 CONNELLY, MARK THOMAS. The Response to Prostitution in the
     Progressive Era. Chapel Hill: University of North Carolina
     Press, 1980. 261 pp.
        Many Americans in the early years of the century con-
     sidered prostitution to be a consequence of the trend for
     women to work in factories and stores and to live away from
     their families. This and other perceptions and misconcep-
     tions, and the antiprostitution campaigns that resulted
     from them, are intelligently discussed in the social and
     intellectual context of the Progressive period in this book.
     Bibliography.

370 CONSUMERS' LEAGUE OF EASTERN PENNSYLVANIA. Occupations for
     Philadelphia Girls. Paper Box Making, 20pp.; Telephone
     Operating, 40 pp.; Bookbinding, 88 pp. Philadelphia:
     Consumers' League of Eastern Pennsylvania, 1913-14.
          These three pamphlets, intended as a basis for voca-
     tional guidance and training, describe in detail the work,
     training, hours, and wages, and assess the advantages and
     disadvantages of each occupation.

371 CONWAY, JILL. "Women Reformers and American Culture, 1870-
     1930." In Our American Sisters: Women in American Life
     and Thought. 2d ed. Edited by Jean E. Friedman and
     William G. Shade, pp. 301-12. Boston: Allyn & Bacon,
     1976.
          Although women progressive reformers such as Jane Addams
     and Lillian Wald were leaders in social reform, Conway be-
     lieves they failed to break the stereotype of the romantic
     women. Their actions were independent, aggressive, and
     rational but they related them to traditional "feminine"
     characteristics such as intuition and natural pacifism.
     Failing to understand the significance of their own lives,
     they lost an opportunity to influence the general percep-
     tion of women's place.

372 COOK, BLANCHE WIESEN. "Female Support Networks and Political
     Activism." In A Heritage of Her Own, edited by Nancy F.
     Cott and Elizabeth H. Pleck, pp. 412-44. New York: Simon
     & Schuster, 1979.
          Cook examines the female friendships of Lillian Wald,
     Jane Addams, Crystal Eastman, and Emma Goldman, and how
     those friendships supported the women in carrying on de-
     manding and difficult careers. Addams and Wald relied
     almost exclusively on women, while Goldman and Eastman also
     had close relationships with men. All drew strength from
     a network of women friends.

373 CRANE, STEPHEN. Maggie: a Girl of the Streets. New York:
     D. Appleton & Co., 1896. 158 pp.
          In Crane's novel of life in the slums, Maggie's longing
     to escape from the sweat shop leads her to prostitution
     and ultimately to suicide.

373a CRANSTON, MARY RANKIN. "How I Bought My Farm." Outlook 100
     (1912):92-96.
          A librarian and writer, Cranston made up her mind to
     leave city life. She bought a farm in New Jersey in 1906,
     and during the next five years developed it into a fruit,
     chicken, and hay farm. (See entry 488.)

374 CRAWFORD, EMILY. "Journalism as a Profession for Women."
     Contemporary Review 64 (1893):362-71.

A journalist describes the perils and pleasures of her profession. (Also cited as entry 57.)

375 CROSS, ROBERT D. "The Philanthropic Contribution of Louisa Lee Schuyler." Social Service Review 35 (1961):290-301.
Brought up in the tradition of "noblesse oblige," Schuyler realized the need for a more systematic approach to charity and social welfare. She was active in the New York State Charities Aid Association and other organizations that helped to establish professional standards for social work.

376 DANIEL, ANNA S. "Condition of the Labor of Women and Children in New York." Journal of Social Science 30 (1892):73-85.
A physician denounces city and state governments for their failure to enforce sanitary, health, and factory laws. The result of this failure is continuance of manufacturing and laundry work in tenements, where disease contaminates the goods and dangerous conditions cause injuries and illness. This paper was presented at the General Meeting of the American Social Science Association, September 1892.

377 DAVIS, ALLEN F. American Heroine: the Life and Legend of Jane Addams. New York: Oxford University Press, 1973. 339 pp.
Davis's understanding of the period and of the settlement movement contributes to his interpretation of the life of one of its most important figures.

378 _____. Spearheads of Reform. New York: Oxford University Press, 1967. 322 pp.
Davis examines the impact of settlement workers on social reform and progressive politics from the 1890s to World War I. Their idealism was applied first to neighborhood improvement, then to municipal reform, and finally to national politics.

379 DAVIS, ELIZABETH LINDSAY. Lifting As They Climb. Washington, D.C.: National Association of Colored Women, 1933. 424 pp.
This official history of the National Association of Colored Women, with a title that speaks volumes, includes information on individual chapters and brief biographies of many women active in the organization, with their portraits. A rich source of information not readily available elsewhere.

380 DE GRAAF, LAWRENCE B. "Race, Sex, and Region: Black Women in the American West, 1850-1920." Pacific Historical Review 49 (1980):285-313.
Black women in the West worked as teachers, nurses, domestic servants, and proprietors of hotels and hairdressing establishments. Few in numbers, they experienced

the social and political effects of race prejudice; the
author finds they were not restricted to a single economic
class.

381   DODGE, GRACE HOADLEY.   What Women Can Earn: Occupations of
      Women and Their Compensations.   Boston: Frederick A.
      Stokes, 1898.   354 pp.   Reprint (microfilm).   In History
      of Women, no. 4918.   New Haven, Conn.:   Research Publica-
      tions, 1975.
          A series of articles describes a great variety of occu-
      pations including typing, portrait painting, goldfish farm-
      ing, dairy farming, and others.

382   DORR, RHETA CHILDE.   What Eight Million Women Want.   Boston:
      Small, Maynard & Co., 1910.   339 pp.
          Women have learned to use their clubs and organizations
      to effect social reforms, from improving parks and play-
      grounds to limiting hours of work.

383   _____.   A Woman of Fifty.   New York: Funk & Wagnalls, 1924.
      451 pp.
          The autobiography of a journalist active in the investi-
      gation of working conditions of women in factories, laun-
      dries, and elsewhere.   Dorr traveled much in England and
      in Russia.   When women's club leaders began to take an
      interest in social reform, she educated the women on the
      need for improvement of factory conditions for women
      workers.

384   DRAKE, WILLIAM.   Sara Teasdale, Woman and Poet.   New York:
      Harper & Row, 1979.   304 pp.
          Sara Teasdale, her biographer says, brought nineteenth-
      century women poets into the twentieth century, incorporat-
      ing into her work the new era's open attitudes about love.
      Teasdale herself struggled with the tensions between work
      and emotional relationships.

384a DREIER, MARY E.   Margaret Dreier Robins, Her Life, Letters,
      and Work.   New York: Island Press Cooperative, 1950.
      278 pp.
          Margaret Dreier Robins was a labor reformer and a leader
      in the National Women's Trade Union League.   This biography
      is based primarily on letters she wrote to her sister, who
      is the author of this book.

385   DREISER, THEODORE.   Sister Carrie.   New York: Doubleday,
      1900.   557 pp.
          In Dreiser's great novel, Carrie comes to Chicago, and
      works briefly in a shoe factory.   Seeking security and com-
      fort, she finds men with money and builds a career as an
      actress.

386 DRINNON, RICHARD. <u>Rebel in Paradise: a Biography of Emma</u>
     <u>Goldman</u>. Chicago: University of Chicago Press, 1961.
     349 pp.
          The anarchist hero Emma Goldman came to America in 1886.
     She became a leader of the movement and an outspoken advo-
     cate of labor and of feminism. Drinnon's biography is ad-
     miring, and surely not the last that will be done. Her own
     version of her life (<u>see</u> entry 409) is more spirited.

387 DuBOIS, W. E. BURGHARDT, ed. <u>The College-Bred Negro: Report</u>
     <u>of a Social Study Made Under the Direction of Atlanta Uni-</u>
     <u>versity</u>. Atlanta: Atlanta University Press, 1900. 115 pp.
          This study surveys black college graduates, their ca-
     reers, and marital status. The tables do not always dif-
     ferentiate between men and women, but some information on
     women graduates is available here.

388 DuBOIS, W. E. B[URGHARDT]. <u>Efforts for Social Betterment</u>
     <u>Among Negro Americans, 1890-1920</u>. Atlanta: Atlanta Uni-
     versity Publications no. 14, 1909. 136 pp.
          This publication, based on information gathered in nine
     Southern cities, reviews institutions such as churches,
     orphanages, settlements, women's clubs, and old people's
     homes.

389 DURAND, JOHN D. <u>The Labor Force in the United States, 1890-</u>
     <u>1960</u>. New York: Gordon & Breach, 1968. 284 pp.
          This thoughtful demographic study considers the social
     implications of changes in the work force over seventy
     years, including the increasing participation of women
     and their higher age at entrance into employment.

390 DYE, NANCY SCHROM. <u>As Equals and As Sisters: Feminism, the</u>
     <u>Labor Movement, and the Women's Trade Union League of New</u>
     <u>York</u>. Columbia and London: University of Missouri Press,
     1980. 200 pp.
          From its founding in 1903 until World War I the New
     York Women's Trade Union League pursued the goal of union
     organization for women workers. Its members, determined
     that a cross-class alliance of women would work, achieved
     a great deal. The organization continued until 1955, al-
     though in different channels. Dye's study gives particular
     attention to the meeting of middle-class and working-class
     women. Bibliography.

391 _____. "Creating a Feminist Alliance: Sisterhood and Class
     Conflict in the New York Women's Trade Union League, 1903-
     1914." <u>Feminist Studies</u> 2 (1975):24-38.
          The New York Women's Trade Union League, formed as a
     coalition between working women and upper-class women, had
     only partial success in bridging the gap between classes.

81

Working women experienced conflict between loyalty to their class and support of the women's movement. League members failed to understand the two facets of the working woman's situation--her exploitation as a worker and her suffering as a woman.

392   EATON, ISABEL. "A Special Report on Domestic Service." In *The Philadelphia Negro*, edited by W. E. B. Dubois, pp. 425-509. Philadelphia: University of Pennsylvania, 1899.
      Ninety-one percent of employed black women in the Seventh Ward of Philadelphia were domestic servants. This study compiles information about wages, age, literacy, health, and employers' opinions about their servants.

393   EDWARDS, RICHARD C. *Contested Terrain: the Transformation of the Workplace in the Twentieth Century*. New York: Basic Books, 1979. 261 pp.
      Beginning with simple worker-owner relationships in small companies, Edwards analyzes the forms of control and the changes in management techniques necessitated by the rise of monopoly capitalism. Technical control (task specificity and threats backed by surplus labor supply) and bureaucratic control make it in the workers' self-interest to be loyal and "good."

394   ELLIOTT, MAUD HOWE, ed. *Art and Handicraft in the Woman's Building of the World's Columbian Exposition, Chicago, 1893*. Paris and New York: Goupil, 1893. 287 pp.
      The Board of Lady Managers of the Woman's Building undertook to mount exhibitions reflecting the work of women around the world. In this volume Bertha Honoré Palmer gives a brief history of the planning of the display; other essays, profusely illustrated, discuss women's work in art, music, literature, handicrafts, and other fields.

395   FELDBERG, ROSLYN. "'Union Fever': Organizing Among Clerical Workers, 1900-1930." *Radical America* 14 (1980):53-67.
      Clerical workers were seen as unorganizable because they were white-collar, native-born, and female, and they did not expect to continue working for a long time. They perceived unions as existing for factory workers. In the early twentieth century stenographers and typists did organize, but participation declined in the 1920s.

395a FERA, DARLA, comp. *Women in American Agriculture, A Selected Bibliography*. Library List 102. Washington, D.C.: National Agricultural Library, 1977. 33 pp. Available from EDRS (ED 157 663).
      This thorough bibliography includes books and articles. The compiler has found many brief articles, both in

agricultural journals and in such publications as <u>Suburban Life</u> and <u>World's Work</u>, which will be useful to researchers.

396 FERBER, EDNA. <u>A Peculiar Treasure</u>. New York: Doubleday, Doran, 1939. 398 pp.
   In this cheerful autobiography Ferber recounts her adventures and travels from her early newspaper days in Appleton, Wisconsin, Milwaukee, and Chicago to her achievements as a writer of fiction and plays.

397 FETHERLING, DALE. <u>Mother Jones, the Miners' Angel: a Portrait</u>. Carbondale: Southern Illinois University Press, 1974. 263 pp.
   This biography takes much of its material from Mother Jones's autobiography (entry 432), but it sets her story in historical perspective. The author considers Mother Jones's role as a folk hero of the trade-union movement.

398 FITZPATRICK, M. LOUISE. <u>The National Organization for Public Health Nursing 1912-1952: Development of a Practice Field</u>. New York: National League for Nursing, 1975. 226 pp.
   Beginning in the late nineteenth century visiting nurses brought health education, preventive care, and nursing of the sick into neighborhoods. Led by Lillian Wald of the Henry Street Settlement, professionals and laypersons interested in widening the availability of public health nursing and establishing professional standards founded this organization.

399 FLEXNER, ELEANOR. <u>Century of Struggle: the Woman's Rights Movement in the United States</u>. Revised ed. Cambridge: Harvard University Press, 1975. 405 pp.
   Flexner's history of the woman's movement includes in its scope both the organization of trade unions and the campaign for suffrage. Bibliography.

400 FLYNN, ELIZABETH GURLEY. <u>The Rebel Girl, an Autobiography: My First Life (1906-1926)</u>. New rev. ed. New York: International Publishers, 1973. 351 pp.
   Flynn describes her life and activities as a socialist and Industrial Workers of the World (IWW) agitator, and gives her own account of the Lawrence strike of 1912 and the Paterson strike of 1913.

401 FONER, PHILIP S. <u>Women and the American Labor Movement, from Colonial Times to the Eve of World War I</u>. New York: Free Press; London: Collier Macmillan, 1979. 621 pp.
   This massive history surveys women's activities in trade union organization, the Women's Trade Union League, and political parties such as the Socialist Party and the Industrial Workers of the World. Extensive bibliography.

402   FULMER, HARRIET. "History of Visiting Nurse Work in America."
       American Journal of Nursing 2 (1902):411-25.
       The author describes the work of the visiting or dis-
       trict nurse and defends the usefulness of such service.
       A list of visiting nurse associations by city, with a
       brief history of each, is included.

403   GALBRAITH, JOHN KENNETH. Economics and the Public Purpose.
       Boston: Houghton Mifflin, 1973. 334 pp.
       Galbraith's analysis of women as a "crypto-servant
       class" in industrial countries is relevant to the study of
       women in the early twentieth century. The spirit of
       Charlotte Perkins Gilman hovers over his proposals for
       "the equitable household" and for reform of consumption
       patterns.

404   GARCIA, MARIO T. "The Chicana in American History: the
       Mexican Women of El Paso, 1880-1920, a Case Study."
       Pacific Historical Review 49 (1980):315-37.
       Mexican women in El Paso most frequently worked as domes-
       tic servants or laundresses in commercial establishments,
       but they also were employed in cigar factories, as clerks,
       and as prostitutes. The author urges further research on
       Chicanas.

405   GARRISON, DEE. Apostles of Culture: the Public Librarian and
       American Society, 1876-1920. New York: The Free Press,
       1979. 319 pp.
       Garrison traces the shaping of the library profession by
       its leaders (especially Melvil Dewey) and the role of the
       public library in the education of immigrants and other
       working-class Americans as well as middle-class readers,
       with particular attention to the relationship of social
       ideals to social needs. She applies the "feminization"
       theory of Ann Douglas (The Feminization of American Culture,
       New York, Alfred A. Knopf, 1977) to the librarian's profes-
       sion, perceiving the entry of large numbers of women as a
       weakening force that held down salaries, diminished their
       political power, and fostered an image of librarians as
       weak and self-effacing.

406   GILMAN, CHARLOTTE PERKINS. The Living of Charlotte Perkins
       Gilman, an Autobiography. New York: Harper & Row, 1975.
       341 pp.
       The author of Women and Economics, whose thinking about
       the need for women's economic independence and the reforms
       that might make it possible influenced feminists in Britain
       as well as in the United States, interprets her own life.
       Her personal experiences, work as a writer and lecturer,
       and theories, all closely interrelated, make this an unusual
       document. Mary Hill's biography (see entry 422) offers an
       interpretation of the autobiography.

407 _____. Women and Economics: the Economic Factor Between Men and Women as a Factor in Social Evolution. Boston: Small, Maynard & Co., 1898. Reprint. New York: Harper & Row, 1966. 356 pp.
      The focus of traditional family life in the private home, Gilman believed, is too narrow, limiting both human ethical growth and economic development. Women must cease to be dependents and take their places in the world of work. This book explains her philosophy of work and describes the society she envisions.

408 GLASGOW, ELLEN. The Woman Within. New York: Harcourt, Brace & Co., 1954. 307 pp.
      Glasgow, a writer who received much acclaim for novels of life in her home state of Virginia, describes in this autobiography her active pursuit of success and her struggles against the isolation of deafness. Marjorie R. Kaufman, in her excellent essay on Glasgow in Notable American Women (entry 476), points out that this account may not be factually reliable, but Glasgow's interpretation of her own life is valuable.

409 GOLDMAN, EMMA. Living My Life. 2 vols. New York: Alfred A. Knopf, 1931.
      Emma Goldman's account of her life as an anarchist, labor leader, and birth-control advocate is more vivid than any historian's so far.

410 GOLDMARK, JOSEPHINE. Fatigue and Efficiency, a Study in Industry. New York: Charities Publication Committee, 1912. 302, 519 pp.
      The physical and mental fatigue caused by long hours, speed, and monotony in factory work wears out workers and imperils the health of future generations. Part 1 studies in detail the problems of fatigue; part 2 reprints four briefs including Muller v. Oregon, by the author and Louis D. Brandeis, submitted in support of laws limiting hours of work.

411 _____. Impatient Crusader: Florence Kelley's Life Story. Urbana: University of Illinois Press, 1953. Reprint. Westport, Conn.: Greenwood Press, 1976. 217 pp.
      The biography of the crusader for protective legislation for women and children concentrates on her work and particularly on the legislative and court battles. Goldmark, a friend and colleague, witnessed or participated in many of the events described.

412 GOODMAN, INEZ. "A Nine-Hour Day for Domestic Servants." The Independent 54 (1902):397-400.

Goodman urges employers to adjust their households and thus enable servants to work a more reasonable schedule, have lives of their own, and preferrably, live in their own homes.

413   GOODMAN, PEARL, and EULAND, ELSA. "The Shirtwaist Trade." Journal of Political Economy 18 (1910):816-28.
The authors review the achievements that followed the shirtwaist-workers' strike of 1909, acknowledging the important role of unions in obtaining and maintaining better working conditions.

414   GORDON, LINDA. Woman's Body, Woman's Right: a Social History of Birth Control in America. New York: Grossman, 1976; Harmondsworth, England: Penguin Books, 1977. 479 pp.
Gordon relates attitudes toward birth control to social and political movements, and shows the relationship of the birth-control movement to changes in women's working lives. She examines the theories of voluntary motherhood and "race suicide." She argues that birth control should not have been made a separate issue, that it is part of a larger social and economic issue.

415   GREER, GERMAINE. The Obstacle Race: the Fortunes of Women Painters and Their Work. New York: Farrar, Straus, Giroux, 1979. 373 pp.
Reviewing women artists since medieval times, this book is sometimes chronological and sometimes genre-oriented. Greer theorizes on why women artists have been overlooked and why few have achieved greatness. This should be a forerunner of more detailed studies; it lacks a bibliography, but has thorough footnotes.

416   GROTZINGER, LAUREL. "The Proto-Feminist Librarian at the Turn of the Century: Two Studies." Journal of Library History, Philosophy, and Comparative Librarianship 10 (1975):195-213.
Katharine Sharp (1865-1914) and Margaret Mann (1873-1960) are presented as examples of strong, dynamic women who entered the "woman's profession" of librarianship to perform active, creative work that had a lasting impact on the profession. As library administrators, pioneers in the organization of library materials, and teachers, they made important contributions to the field.

417   GUTMAN, HERBERT G. Work, Culture and Society in Industrializing America: Essays in American Working-Class and Social History. New York: Alfred A. Knopf, 1976. 343 pp.
Immigrants to the United States, expecting to find a working people's country, found instead the actuality of class division and industrial rulers. Gutman discusses the social process of Americanization, and of adjusting people to work habits and discipline that fit the factory schedule.

418   HAREVEN, TAMARA K. "Family Time and Industrial Time: Family
      and Work in a Planned Corporation Town 1900-1924." <u>Journal
      of Urban History</u> 1 (1975):365-89.
            Observations on the interaction of family and corpora-
      tion are based on a study of French-Canadian immigrants in
      the textile mill town of Manchester, New Hampshire. Trac-
      ing the networks of extended families and friends through
      whom the immigrants found work and housing as they moved
      south, Hareven shows how the family, particularly before
      World War I, enabled its members to have greater flexibil-
      ity in choosing jobs and moving in and out of the workforce.
      Of particular interest is the discussion of differing roles
      and expectations of sons and daughters.

419   HAREVEN, TAMARA K., and LANDENBACH, RANDOLPH. <u>Amoskeag, Life
      and Work in an American Factory-City</u>. New York: Pantheon
      Books, 1978. 395 pp.
            The Amoskeag Manufacturing Company, a textile factory in
      Manchester, New Hampshire, started in 1837, and closed in
      1975. Manchester, like some other New England mill towns,
      was a planned city, and most workers lived in company hous-
      ing. Many of the workers were French Canadians lured by
      advertisements in Quebec newspapers. This collection of
      interviews with men and women who worked in the mill (many
      of whose parents worked in the mill) presents a picture
      composed of detailed recollections--how they started at
      the mill, what the work was like, family life, friendships,
      changes.

420   HARRISON, CYNTHIA, ed. <u>Women in American History: A Bibliog-
      raphy</u>. Santa Barbara, Calif. and Oxford, England: American
      Bibliographical Center, Clio Press, 1979. 374 pp.
            This bibliography contains abstracts of articles in
      periodicals and collections published between 1963 and
      1976; most are taken from <u>America: History and Life</u>.
      Author and subject indexes.

420a HATHAWAY, GRACE. <u>Fate Rides a Tortoise: a Biography of Ellen
      Spencer Mussey</u>. Chicago: John C. Winston, 1937. 204 pp.
            Mussey took over her husband's law practice while he was
      ill. Subsequently she was admitted to the bar at the age
      of forty-two. In 1898 she founded the Washington College
      of Law, the first law school established primarily for women.
      The few quotations from Mussey's letters suggest a witty,
      bright, and determined woman, but the biography offers lit-
      tle interpretation of her life.

421   HILL, JOSEPH A. <u>Women in Gainful Occupations 1870 to 1920, a
      Study of the Trend of Recent Changes in the Numbers, Occupa-
      tional Distribution, and Family Relationship of Women Re-
      ported in the Census as Following a Gainful Occupation</u>.

United States Bureau of the Census, Census Monographs IX.
Washington, D.C.: U.S. Government Printing Office, 1929.
416 pp.
 This invaluable study of all aspects of women's work is
accompanied by 173 detailed tables of statistics.

422 HILL, MARY A. Charlotte Perkins Gilman: the Making of a
Radical Feminist, 1860–1896. Philadelphia: Temple University Press, 1980. 362 pp.
 The first volume of this projected two-volume biography
is a good companion for Gilman's autobiography (see entry
406). It offers an interpretation of that work as well as
additional information. It is a well-written, sensitive
study of an interesting feminist.

423 HINDING, ANDREA, ed. Women's History Sources: a Guide to
Archives and Manuscript Collections in the United States.
2 vols. New York and London: R. R. Bowker Co., 1979.
 This guide to primary sources identifies over 18,000
collections pertaining to United States women. The entries,
arranged by state, city, and institution, include information on collection size, types of documents, and dates covered, access information, and guides to the collections.
Volume 2 is an extensive index to volume 1. Although there
are some omissions and errors, the guide is of tremendous
value, particularly in locating little-known collections.

424 HIRATA, LUCIE CHENG. "Free, Indentured, Enslaved: Chinese
Prostitutes in Nineteenth-Century America." Signs: Journal
of Women in Culture and Society 5 (1979):3–29.
 Hirata studies prostitution in California and the exploitation of Chinese prostitutes as laborers in a semifeudal
system in which both sex and race exploitation took place.
Describing the methods of bringing Chinese women to America
as prostitutes and the conditions under which they worked,
she points out reasons the exploitation was possible: the
connection between Chinese emigrant organizations and California Chinese merchants; white racism; and the small proportion of white women in California. After 1870 Chinese
prostitution declined as white women immigrants arrived and
crusades against prostitution took place.

425 HOBSON, ELIZABETH CHRISTOPHERS. Recollections of a Happy Life.
New York and London: G. P. Putnam's Sons, 1916. 258 pp.
 Having participated in the establishment of the Bellevue
Training School for nurses in New York and lived in Latin
America, Mrs. Hobson toured the South, visiting schools
for blacks on behalf of the Slater Fund.

426 HOGGAN, FRANCES. "Negro Women in America." Englishwoman 12
(October–December 1911):24–38.

The author admires the achievements of black women since
the Civil War, particularly their work as doctors and
teachers. She observes their natural aptitude for child
care, and their respect for the work of the homemaker.
Particular attention is given to Georgia Washington,
founder of a school at Mount Meigs, Alabama.

427   HOLT, RACKHAM. <u>Mary McLeod Bethune, a Biography</u>. Garden City,
       N.Y.: Doubleday & Co., 1964. 306 pp.
       After completing her studies at the Moody Bible Insti-
       tute in 1895, Bethune became a teacher. In 1904 she founded
       the Daytona Normal and Industrial School for Girls in Flor-
       ida (now Bethune-Cookman College). <u>Notable American Women</u>
       describes her as "the most influential black woman in the
       United States through more than three decades."

428   HOWARD, GEORGE ELLIOTT. "Changed Ideals and Status of the
       Family and the Public Activities of Women." <u>Annals of the</u>
       <u>American Academy of Political and Social Science</u> 56 (1914):
       27-37.
       The home, Howard says, is no longer a woman's profession;
       the family is now an equal arrangement, and fathers should
       take a greater part in child rearing.

428a   HUNT, CAROLINE L. <u>The Life of Ellen H. Richards</u>. Boston:
       Whitcomb & Barrows, 1912. 328 pp.
       Ellen Richards was a leader in the development of the
       field of home economics. She studied chemistry at Vassar
       and Massachusetts Institute of Technology. At the Chicago
       World's Fair she set up the Rumford Kitchen to demonstrate
       nutritious meals. This contemporary biography is the most
       complete one available.

429   HUNT, VILMA. <u>The Health of Women at Work, a Bibliography</u>.
       University Program on Women, Occasional Papers, no. 2.
       Chicago: Northwestern University, 1977. 173 pp.
       The historical section gives useful references.

430   ICHIOKA, YUJI. "Amerika Nadeshiko: Japanese Immigrant Women
       in the United States, 1900-1924." <u>Pacific Historical Review</u>
       49 (1980):339-57.
       Many Japanese women who came to the United States in
       this period came as "picture brides." They worked with
       their husbands in labor camps, on farms, and in small busi-
       nesses, in addition to maintaining households under primi-
       tive living conditions.

431   JACOBY, ROBIN MILLER. "Feminism and Class Consciousness in
       the British and American Women's Trade Union Leagues, 1890-
       1925." In <u>Liberating Women's History</u>, edited by Bernice A.
       Carroll, pp. 137-60. Urbana: University of Illinois Press,
       1976.

Women met across class lines in the Women's Trade Union
Leagues, but the concept of sisterhood of all women did not
always overcome the consciousness of class differences.
Jacoby studies the organization, education, and legislation
programs of the League in the United States and Great Britain, with particular attention to its relationship to the
suffrage movement.

432   JONES, MARY H. Autobiography of Mother Jones. Edited by Mary
       Field Parton. Introduction by Clarence Darrow. Chicago:
       Charles H. Kerr & Company, 1925. 242 pp.
           Mother Jones's life was a series of dramatic encounters
       between her and the miners and managers of the coal fields.
       She has a vigorous style and a strong sense of herself as
       hero. Lacking in connecting information, the autobiography
       needs to be supplemented by other material. (See entries
       334 and 397.)

432a   Journal of Home Economics. 3 (October 1911).
           This entire issue is a memorial to Ellen Swallow Richards,
       the leader of the home economics movement who died in 1911.
       A series of brief articles describe activities and institu-
       tions in which Richards had been a part, including the New
       England Kitchen in Boston, which was designed to demonstrate
       nutritious eating for working people but became more popu-
       lar with the middle class; programs at the University of
       Chicago, the University of Tennessee, and Johns Hopkins
       University, the National Home Economics Association, and
       many others. For a biography of Richards see entry 428a.

433   KATZMAN, DAVID M. Seven Days a Week: Women and Domestic Ser-
       vice in Industrializing America. New York: Oxford Univer-
       sity Press, 1978. 374 pp.
           This excellent sociological-historical study surveys
       women in domestic service from 1870 to 1920, a period of in-
       dustrialization and urbanization and of transition from the
       live-in to the live-out servant. In addition to analyzing
       statistical patterns, the author has interesting observa-
       tions on the tendency of employers to translate their sus-
       picions into racial characteristics attributed to servants'
       ethnic groups; the preference of employers for a "personal"
       relationship with servants; and other aspects of the
       mistress-servant dialogue. Bibliography.

434   KELLOR, FRANCES A. Out of Work, a Study of Employment Agen-
       cies: Their Treatment of the Unemployed, and Their Influ-
       ence Upon Homes and Business. New York and London:
       G. P. Putnam's Sons, 1905. 292 pp.
           Investigators visited employment agencies posing as em-
       ployers or as women seeking employment. They report on
       practices, fees, treatment of clients, and frauds. A major

portion of the book is concerned with domestic service
agencies, but there are chapters on agencies for professionals and office workers, free agencies sponsored by
churches and other organizations, and legislation.
    In a revised edition (1915) Kellor increased her criti-
cism of existing services and recommended a national system
of employment bureaus and unemployment insurance.

435   KELLY, FLORENCE FINCH. Flowing Stream: the Story of Fifty-
      Six Years in American Newspaper Life. New York: E. P.
      Dutton & Co., 1939. 571 pp.
          Kelly's career in journalism began in Chicago when she
      was twenty-three. She was the first woman on the staff of
      the Boston Globe. She married and had a child, and in 1906
      began a long association with the New York Times, where much
      of her work was on the Book Review. She also wrote novels.
      Her autobiography is a frank and matter-of-fact account of
      her life and career, with observations on the newspaper
      world and on American politics.

436   KENNEALLY, JAMES J. "Women and Trade Unions 1870-1920: the
      Quandary of the Reformer." Labor History 14 (1973):42-55.
          Trade union leaders in the United States believed that
      women should be unionized for their own protection and for
      the security of the men with whom they competed for jobs.
      At the same time they were convinced that women belonged
      at home and were caught in the conflict between these ideas.

437   _____. Women in American Trade Unions. St. Albans, Vt.:
      Eden Press, 1978. 240 pp.
          This history of women's trade unionism includes biogra-
      phies of important women in the movement.

438   KENNEDY, DAVID M. Birth Control in America: the Career of
      Margaret Sanger. New Haven and London: Yale University
      Press, 1970. 320 pp.
          This biography skillfully sets the life and career of
      the leader of the birth-control movement in the context of
      her time. Bibliography.

439   KENNEDY, SUSAN ESTABROOK. If All We Did Was Weep at Home: a
      History of White Working-Class Women in America. Blooming-
      ton: Indiana University Press, 1979. 331 pp.
          This perceptive, well-written history places working-
      class women in historical context and in their relation to
      women of other classes. An excellent bibliography of pub-
      lished and unpublished sources.

440   KERR, THOMAS J., IV. "The New York Factory Investigating
      Commission and the Minimum Wage Movement." Labor History
      12 (1971):373-91.

The New York Factory Investigating Commission was respon-
sible for the most extensive wage study in the United States
in the early twentieth century. It brought to public attention the arguments in favor of a minimum wage.

441   KESSLER-HARRIS, ALICE. "Organizing the Unorganizable: Three
Jewish Women and Their Union." Labor History 17 (1976):
5-23.
      Pauline Newman, Fannia Cohn, and Rose Pessotta, three
organizers for the International Ladies Garment Workers
Union, illustrate the conflicts experienced by women working for the union. Their need for independence was threat-
ened by the Jewish community's pressure to marry and have
children. All of them had mixed emotions about the inter-
vention of middle-class women. The author examines their
reliance on friendships with other women or on relationships with men for support.

442   _____. "'Where Are the Organized Women Workers?'" In A
Heritage of Her Own, edited by Nancy F. Cott and Elizabeth H.
Pleck, pp. 343-66. New York: Simon & Schuster, 1979.
      The author studies the reasons behind women's participa-
tion or lack of participation in trade unions early in the
twentieth century: why men's unions discouraged women from
joining; the influence of the Women's Trade Union League;
the attitudes of women toward their own work; and the relationship of women workers to employers and to men workers.

443   _____. "Women's Wage Work as Myth and History." Labor History 19 (1978):287-307.
      In a review essay that comments on several reprints of
studies done in the late nineteenth and early twentieth
centuries as well as on some recent writing on women's
work, the author remarks that the earlier studies accepted
assumptions about women's family role that affected their
findings on women's wage work. Looking at women's work
from the perspective of labor market segmentation theory,
or dual labor market theory, brings different--and inter-
esting--results.

444   KEY, ELLEN. The Woman Movement. New York: G. P. Putnam's
Sons, 1912. 224 pp.
      Key's book, originally published in Sweden in 1909,
evaluates the changes in women's relationship to society
that have resulted from the feminist movement. She believes single women have benefitted both in wider opportunities and in better family relationships. She discusses
changes in mother-daughter relationships and marital and
maternal roles. Critical of the "amaternal" position of
feminists such as Charlotte Perkins Gilman, she endorses
old-fashioned motherhood.

445   KLACZYNSKA, BARBARA. "Why Women Work: a Comparison of Various Groups--Philadelphia, 1910-1930." <u>Labor History</u> 17 (1976):73-87.

A comparison of women of different ethnic groups shows varying attitudes toward working and toward types of work. Poles took boarders, Italians did home-work, and blacks went into domestic service through lack of other opportunities. Women were more likely to work after they had been in this country for a while, and were likely to leave the work force as they moved into the middle class.

446   KLEINBERG, SUSAN J. "Technology and Women's Work: the Lives of Working Class Women in Pittsburgh, 1870-1900." <u>Labor History</u> 17 (1976):58-72.

Women, for whom there were few jobs in Pittsburgh, managed households and family finances. Housekeeping was difficult because of the lack of city services such as paved roads and piped water in working-class sections. Technological innovations (refrigeration, indoor plumbing, etc.) that made housework easier were expensive, so women's labor was substituted. Kleinberg suggests that women felt more deprived because they knew these things existed.

447   KNEELAND, GEORGE. <u>Commercialized Prostitution in New York City</u>. New York: Century Co., 1913. 334 pp.

The Bureau of Social Hygiene formed in 1911 issued this report that deals with all facets of organized prostitution: places, people (exploiters, prostitutes, madams, and customers), law enforcement, and reform organizations. A chapter by Katherine Bement Davis analyzes the background and histories of prostitutes in the New York State Reformatory at Bedford Hills.

448   KRADITOR, AILEEN S. <u>The Ideas of the Woman Suffrage Movement 1890-1920</u>. New York: Columbia University Press, 1965. 313 pp.

As there is no "ideology" of the suffrage movement, Kraditor studies the thinking of its national leaders, and identifies some interesting, if not always laudable, ideas. Southern suffragists were antiblack, Northern suffragists were antiimmigrant. Reformers like Jane Addams and Florence Kelley believed suffrage was a means to bring about social justice.

449   <u>Labor History</u>. 1960-

An annual bibliography in this journal provides a good source of reference for work in the field of labor history.

450   <u>Labor in the Twentieth Century</u>. Edited by John T. Dunlop and Walter Galenson. New York, San Francisco, and London: Academic Press, 1978. 329 pp.

Each of the five essays considers one country's changes in size and composition of the labor force, trade unions, wages and salaries, and the role of the state and legislation. For perspectives on women in the labor force, 1900-14, related to later developments, see the chapters by Walter Galenson and Robert S. Smith, "The United States," pp. 11-84; and A. W. J. Thompson and L. C. Hunter, "Great Britain," pp. 85-146.

451 LAGEMANN, ELLEN CONDLIFFE. <u>A Generation of Women: Education in the Lives of Progressive Reformers</u>. Cambridge: Harvard University Press, 1979. 207 pp.
    Examining the lifelong education of five women (Grace Dodge, Maud Nathan, Lillian Wald, Leonora O'Reilly, and Rose Schneiderman) Lagemann finds that parental teaching and mentors in adult life were the most important influences on their learning. A chapter on each woman gives biographical information and raises some provocative questions for future researchers. The conclusion reviews similarities and differences and observes the interclass learning that all of them experienced in their work.

452 LASCH, CHRISTOPHER. <u>The New Radicalism in America 1889-1963: The Intellectual as a Social Type</u>. New York: Alfred A. Knopf, 1965. 349 pp.
    The author interprets radicalism through the lives of intellectuals; biography is the center of his analysis. Among his subjects are Jane Addams and Mabel Dodge Luhan, two women whose careers differ widely. The fictional portrayals of Robert Herrick and the ideas of Charlotte Perkins Gilman also enter into Lasch's study of the "new woman" and her problems.

452a LASELLE, MARY A. <u>The Young Woman Worker</u>. Boston: Pilgrim Press, 1914. 189 pp.
    This didactic book advises young women working in offices and shops as to manners, clean habits, and ways of maintaining physical and mental health. In the illustrative anecdotes, employers promote the faithful and well-behaved, though they may say, "Your example and influence in this store cannot be estimated in terms of salary!" (p. 167). The book's message is "Force yourself to be ever sweet-tempered, polite, and obliging" (p. 44).

453 LASH, JOSEPH P. <u>Helen and Teacher: the Story of Helen Keller and Anne Sullivan Macy</u>. New York: Delacorte Press/ Seymour Lawrence, 1980. 811 pp.
    In a dual biography, Lash examines the complicated relationship between the blind and deaf Helen Keller and her remarkable teacher, Anne Sullivan Macy. Trained and educated by Macy, Helen Keller graduated from Radcliffe in

1904. Their work together had great impact on the education of the blind and deaf.

454 LERNER, GERDA. The Majority Finds Its Past: Placing Women
in History. New York and Oxford: Oxford University Press,
1979. 256 pp.
In a collection of essays Lerner examines several areas
of women's history in the United States. Of special interest are her discussions of black women, which include an
essay on historiography, one on women's clubs, and one on
interaction between black and white women.

455 LEUPP, CONSTANCE D. "The Shirtwaist Makers' Strike." Survey
23 (1909):383-86.
In a firsthand account of the strike, the author criticizes the police for curtailing first-amendment rights of
the picketers.

456 LEVINE, DANIEL. Jane Addams and the Liberal Tradition.
Madison: State Historical Society of Wisconsin, 1971.
277 pp.
The author of this intellectual biography believes that
Addams's most important work was that of "publicist and
persuader," seeking permanent improvement through change
in the environment.

457 LITOFF, JUDY BARRETT. American Midwives 1860 to the Present.
Westport, Conn. and London: Greenwood Press, 1978. 197 pp.
In 1900 midwives attended one-half of all births in the
United States; in 1973, 99.3 percent of babies were delivered by physicians. In the early part of the century midwives were found chiefly among immigrants and blacks, and
in rural areas. Proponents of midwifery argued that trained
midwives could reduce infant mortality, and sought training
programs. Doctors who wanted to raise the status of obstet-
rics fostered the notion that midwives were ignorant and
dirty. (See Jean Donnison, Midwives and Medical Men,
entry 77, for the British parallel.)

458 LITOFF, JUDY BARRETT, and LITOFF, HAL. "Working Women in
Maine: a Note on Sources." Labor History 17 (1976):88-95.
This is a useful guide, particularly to unpublished
sources.

459 LUBOVE, RAY. The Professional Altruist: the Emergence of
Social Work as a Career 1880-1930. Cambridge: Harvard
University Press, 1965. 291 pp.
The idea of social work as a profession grew from
nineteenth-century volunteer settlement work. The first
formal training school was established in New York in 1898.
Lubove traces the development of the profession, the

introduction of theory, and the establishment of specific
types of social work practice.

460 LYND, STAUGHTON. "Jane Addams and the Radical Impulse."
   Commentary 32 (July 1961):54-59.
       Before the First World War, Jane Addams and her asso-
   ciates believed that reforms could be achieved by gathering
   facts and proving the need for legislation. Always ready
   to act on her convictions, Addams worked within the system
   until her pacifism forced her to an unequivocally radical
   stand on the war.

461 MACARTHUR, MARY R. "The Secretary in America." Women's Trade
   Union Review 66 (July 1907):7-12.
       The British labor leader describes her travels in the
   United States; she visited New York, Philadelphia, and
   Boston, but gives most of her attention to Chicago and
   the Industrial Exhibition there.

462 McGOVERN, JAMES. "The American Woman's Pre-World War I Freedom in Manners and Morals." Journal of American History 55
   (1968):315-33.
       McGovern documents a revolution in manners and morals
   beginning about 1910; he rejects the idea that the new
   freedom for women was a postwar phenomenon. Finding much
   of his evidence in advertising and in fiction, he points
   out that the car, the telephone, and the "job and kitchen
   revolution" led to more liberated behavior and dress in the
   years preceding World War I.

463 McKINLEY, EDWARD H. Marching to Glory: the History of the
   Salvation Army in the United States of America, 1880-1980.
   New York: Harper & Row, 1980. 286 pp.
       Women were active in the Salvation Army from its begin-
   nings. From 1896 to 1903 Emma Booth-Tucker shared the
   leadership of the American organization with her husband,
   Frederick; they established hotels for working women during
   this period. After Emma's death, her sister, Evangeline
   Booth, came from England to rule as Commander, a position
   she held for thirty years.

464 MAGNUSON, NORRIS. Salvation in the Slums: Evangelical Social
   Work 1865-1920. Metuchen, N.J.: Scarecrow Press, 1977.
   299 pp.
       This thoughtful study goes beyond the stereotype and
   reveals the contributions of evangelical groups to social
   reform: homes for working girls, farms for resettlement of
   the urban poor, employment offices, and assistance to pris-
   oners and exprisoners. Blacks, ethnic minorities, and women
   were included both as workers and as recipients of service
   under the principle of equality of all people.

465   MANN, ARTHUR. <u>Yankee Reformers in the Urban Age</u>. Cambridge:
       Harvard University Press, 1954. 314 pp.
            The theories of social reform examined here, which de-
       veloped in Boston between 1880 and 1900, influenced settle-
       ments and other reform activities. Mann discusses Nicholas
       Paine Gilman's Social Gospel and the Christian Socialist
       Movement of W. D. P. Bliss and Vida Scudder.

466   MARKS, GEOFFREY, and BEATTY, WILLIAM K. <u>Women in White, Their
       Role as Doctors Through the Ages</u>. New York: Charles
       Scribner's Sons, 1972. 239 pp.
            An introductory survey of the history of women in medi-
       cine, this discusses their entrance into medical schools in
       the nineteenth century, and their difficulties in procuring
       internships and beginning practice. Brief biographies of
       such physicians as Emily Dunning Barringer and Alice
       Hamilton are included.

467   MARTIN, GEORGE. <u>Madam Secretary: Frances Perkins</u>. Boston:
       Houghton Mifflin, 1976. 589 pp.
            Frances Perkins became interested in social reform while
       she was a student at Mount Holyoke College where she heard
       Florence Kelley speak. After her graduation in 1902, she
       supported herself by teaching and spent her vacations in
       settlement work. In 1910 she became secretary of the New
       York Consumers' League and began a career in public service
       as a lobbyist for legislation limiting hours of work in
       Albany, where she met Al Smith. These early years were
       important in the development of the woman who became the
       first female cabinet member in 1933.

468   MEYER, ANNIE NATHAN, ed. <u>Woman's Work in America</u>. New York:
       H. Holt & Co., 1891. Reprint. New York: Arno Press,
       1972. 457 pp.
            This collection on the history of women's education and
       women's work includes essays on professions, politics, in-
       dustry and philanthropy, and technical training. Alice
       Hyneman Rhine discusses the Women's Exchange as an outlet
       for women's crafts. Laudatory and positive in tone, the
       book was intended to stimulate other women by offering
       examples.

469   MITCHELL, S. WEIR. <u>Doctor and Patient</u>. Philadelphia:
       J. B. Lippincott Co., 1904. 177 pp.
            Dr. Mitchell, famous for his rest-cure treatment of
       nervous women, reflects on doctor-patient relationships
       and on women's health. He is not enthusiastic about higher
       education for women, and believes some careers "inevitably
       lessen her attractiveness;" but he advocates exercise and
       outdoor camping for them.

470   MODELL, JOHN, and HAREVEN, TAMARA K. "Urbanization and the Malleable Household: an Examination of Boarding and Lodging in American Families." Journal of Marriage and the Family 35 (1973):467-79.
      The authors analyze statistics to identify the social and economic position of lodgers and the families that took them. They conclude that boarding provided a surrogate family rather than a contribution to family breakdown.

471   MONROE, HARRIET. A Poet's Life: Seventy Years in a Changing World. New York: Macmillan, 1938. 488 pp.
      The founder of Poetry magazine describes her career as poet, journalist, art critic (she reviewed the Armory exhibition when it came to Chicago in 1913), and editor.

472   MONTGOMERY, LOUISE. The American Girl in the Stockyards District. Chicago: University of Chicago Press, 1913. 70 pp.
      Sponsored by the University of Chicago Settlement, this study surveys American-born daughters of immigrant parents, collecting and analyzing information about attitudes toward education, relationship between years of completed education and employment and earnings, and conflicts between daughters and parents. The girls include a group under sixteen years old, and a group of seventeen- and eighteen-year-olds. The younger girls found work in factories and domestic service, while the older ones frequently held office jobs. The study gives a sympathetic account of the perceptions of immigrants and their children about their roles and behavior. See Tamara Hareven's "Family Time and Industrial Time" (entry 418) and Margaret F. Byington's Homestead (entry 364).

473   MOORE, R. LAURENCE. "The Spiritualist Medium: a Study of Female Professionalism in Victorian America." American Quarterly 27 (1975):200-221.
      The profession of spiritual medium became identified as a women's profession, although there were male mediums. Characteristics of passivity, self-sacrifice, and frail health were necessary to a medium, and these were accepted as female characteristics. The belief in manipulation by spirit voices offered an escape from boredom and conventional behavior. This is an interesting examination of a little-studied occupation.

474   NEIDLE, CECYLE S. American Immigrant Women. Boston: Twayne, 1975. 312 pp.
      This history of European immigrants is at times merely a recital of achievements, but the chapter on immigrant wives and mothers describes both urban and rural settlers from many countries.

475   NEVERDON-MORTON, CYNTHIA. "The Black Woman's Struggle for
       Equality in the South, 1895-1925." In The Afro-American
       Woman: Struggles and Images, edited by Sharon Harley and
       Rosalyn Terborg-Penn, pp. 43-57. New York: Kennikat Press,
       1978.
           Middle-class black women's clubs worked to establish
       educational and social programs in their communities. Al-
       though some integrated organizations existed, the local,
       separate groups were the strongest in this period. (See
       entry 454.)

476   Notable American Women 1607-1950, a Biographical Dictionary.
       3 vols. Edited by Edward T. James, Janet Wilson James, and
       Paul S. Boyer. Cambridge and London: Harvard University
       Press, 1971.
       Notable American Women: the Modern Period: a Biographical
       Dictionary. Edited by Barbara Sicherman and Carol Hurd
       Green with Ilene Kantrov and Harriette Walker. Cambridge
       and London: Harvard University Press, 1980. 773 pp.
           These volumes form a major reference source for the
       lives of American women. Signed biographical essays are
       accompanied by notes on research sources. The original
       work includes women who died before 1951; the supplementary
       volume includes women who died between 1951 and 1975.

477   O'NEILL, WILLIAM L. Divorce in the Progressive Era. New
       Haven: Yale University Press, 1967. 295 pp.
           Public concern about divorce was intense during the
       early years of the twentieth century. O'Neill examines
       the theories behind the movements for and against divorce,
       and the relationship of this concern to women's increasing
       participation in industry and the professions. Bibliography.

478   _____. Everyone Was Brave: a History of Feminism in America.
       Chicago: Quadrangle Books, 1971. 379 pp.
           This account of the history of feminism and the suffrage
       movement examines organizations, leaders, and philosophies.
       O'Neill's thesis is that concentration on suffrage weakened
       the movement, causing it to abandon broader goals of re-
       structuring society and the family.

479   _____. The Woman Movement: Feminism in the United States and
       England. London: George Allen & Unwin; New York: Barnes
       and Noble, 1969. 208 pp.
           Approximately half the book is devoted to a succinct,
       comparative history of feminism in England and in the
       United States. The remainder is a collection of documents
       dating from 1838 to 1929. O'Neill's evaluation of the
       strengths and weaknesses of the movement gives particular
       attention to the various reform efforts in which feminists
       engaged, such as the Consumers' League, the Women's Trade
       Union League, and the temperance movement. Bibliography.

480   O'SULLIVAN, JUDITH, and GALLICK, ROSEMARY. Workers and Allies:
      Female Participation in the American Trade Union Movement,
      1824-1976. Washington, D.C.: Smithsonian Institution
      Press, 1976. 96 pp.
            This catalogue of a Smithsonian exhibition includes a
      brief history of women in the trade unions, a chronology,
      and biographies of women important to the movement.
      Bibliography.

481   PACKARD, ESTHER. A Study of the Living Conditions of Self-
      Supporting Women in New York City. New York: Metropolitan
      Board of the Young Women's Christian Association, 1915.
      96 pp.
            Nonprofit homes for girls, furnished rooms, and boarding
      arrangements with families are included in this survey.
      Statistics and information on occupations and wages of
      girls in each type of accommodation are accompanied by
      observations on their advantages and disadvantages as per-
      ceived by the residents and by the investigators. The in-
      vestigators recommend "socialized apartment houses" (private
      apartments with food service and some housekeeping service)
      for women similar to those already provided for men.

482   PALMER, FANNY PURDY. "Does the Modern Extension of Women's
      Industrial Activities Benefit Mankind Generally?" Proceed-
      ings of the Ninth Annual Convention of the International
      Association of Factory Inspectors, Providence, Rhode Island,
      3-5 September 1895, pp. 49-58.
            Palmer answers her question in the affirmative. Women's
      employment makes them better prepared for marriage, does
      not affect health adversely, has encouraged legislation to
      improve working conditions, and has increased the supply of
      teachers.

483   PATTERSON, JAMES T. "Mary Dewson and the American Minimum
      Wage Movement." Labor History 5 (1964):134-52.
            As director of the women's parole department of the
      Massachusetts industrial school system from 1900 to 1912,
      Mary Dewson became interested in the causes of delinquency
      among girls. Her investigation convinced her that poverty
      and immorality were related, and that the parole system was
      not an effective means of reform. Believing that the solu-
      tion lay in a minimum wage law, she began a long-term cam-
      paign for the passage of such laws, first in Massachusetts
      and later across the nation, working in close cooperation
      with the Consumers' League.

484   PETTENGILL, LILLIAN. "Toilers of the Home, a College Woman's
      Experience as a Domestic Servant." Everybody's Magazine
      8 (1903):273-79, 375-84, 471-80, 561-68.

A graduate of Mount Holyoke describes her experiences
working as a servant under an assumed identity, her personal relationships with employers, and her attempts to
learn necessary skills, such as cooking. Her conclusion
emphasizes the need for a more businesslike arrangement
between mistress and servant.

485   PINZER, MAIMIE. The Maimie Papers. Edited by Ruth Rosen and
      Sue Davidson. Old Westbury, N.Y.: The Feminist Press,
      1977. 439 pp.
          Maimie, a former prostitute, corresponded with Fanny
      Quincy Howe from 1910 to 1922. During that period she
      learned secretarial skills and organized a business pro-
      viding clerical services. Her letters reflect on social
      distinctions among prostitutes, on why girls become prosti-
      tutes, on the economic alternatives (including marriage),
      and on her own values and attitudes.

486   PLECK, ELIZABETH HAFKIN. Black Migration and Poverty: Boston
      1865-1900. New York: Academic Press, 1979. 239 pp.
          This careful study of Boston in the post-Civil War years
      finds very different social attitudes and aspirations among
      native Bostonian blacks and immigrants from the South.
      Native Bostonians aspired to upward mobility and a greater
      degree of integration, while the Southerners were more
      likely to stay in their own group. Racial barriers oper-
      ated against both groups to keep them in low-paid, unskilled,
      temporary work. Of particular interest in the study of work-
      ing women is the chapter on families. Bibliographic essay.

487   _____. "A Mother's Wages: Income Earning Among Married
      Italian and Black Women, 1896-1911." In A Heritage of Her
      Own, edited by Nancy F. Cott and Elizabeth H. Pleck, pp.
      367-92. New York: Simon & Schuster, 1979.
          Drawing on Labor Bureau studies done in 1896 and 1911,
      the author finds that black women participated in the labor
      force at a much higher rate than Italian women. Pleck sug-
      gests that black women raised their children to be more
      independent, that they were ambitious for their children's
      education, and that they wanted to share with their husbands
      the burden of wage-earning.

488   PRINGLE, ELIZABETH WATRIS [Patience Pennington]. A Woman Rice
      Planter. New York: Macmillan, 1914. 450 pp.
          The author, owner and manager of two rice plantations in
      a remote part of South Carolina, describes in diary form
      her experiences from 1903 to 1907: managing crops, train-
      ing horses, raising chickens in an incubator, and supervis-
      ing a staff of former slaves and children of former slaves.
      Far from relatives and friends, and almost without money,
      she rents out acreage for a share of the crop, and deals

with crises as they come. Originally published serially
in the New York Sun, this is both dramatic and informative.

489   RANDALL, MERCEDES M. Improper Bostonian: Emily Greene Balch.
      New York: Twayne, 1964. 475 pp.
          Emily Balch (1867-1961) began her career as a settlement
      worker in Boston. She taught economics at Wellesley for
      twenty years until her pacifism and radical economic views
      led the trustees to terminate her appointment, and she
      worked for world peace through two wars. She was awarded
      the Nobel Peace Prize in 1946. Among her friends and asso-
      ciates were Mary Simkhovitch, Jane Addams, and Florence
      Kelley.

490   RICHARDSON, DOROTHY. The Long Day: the Story of a New York
      Working Girl, as Told by Herself. New York: Century Co.,
      1906. 309 pp.
          A middle-class woman describes her experiences working
      in New York as a seamstress and maker of artificial flowers.
      She portrays working girls as coarse, vulgar, and apathetic,
      with a few shining exceptions; this picture drew criticism
      when the book was published.

491   RICHMOND, MARY E. The Long View: Papers and Addresses.
      Selected and edited with biographical information by
      Joanna C. Colcord. New York: Russell Sage Foundation,
      1930. 646 pp.
          Mary Richmond invented the case method of training social
      workers. The most interesting papers in this collection of
      her writings deal with the need for professional schools.

492   RODGERS, DANIEL T. The Work Ethic in Industrial America,
      1850-1920. Chicago: University of Chicago Press, 1978.
      300 pp.
          Examining efforts to apply the work ethic to the altered
      working conditions of industrialization, Rodgers discusses
      middle-class ideals about work, incentives offered to fac-
      tory workers, and the fears raised by the increasingly
      mechanical nature of work. Chapter 7, "Idle Womanhood:
      Feminist Versions of the Work Ethic" (pp. 182-209), is an
      interesting discussion of the work ethic and feminism:
      particular attention is given to Charlotte Perkins Gilman
      and Harriet Beecher Stowe. The author comments on the con-
      flicts experienced by middle-class feminists trying to rec-
      oncile their idealized view of work with the real life of
      women factory workers.

493   ROSSITER, MARGARET W. "Women Scientists Before 1920." In
      Dynamos and Virgins Revisited: Women and Technological
      Change in History, an Anthology, edited by Martha Moore
      Trescott, pp. 120-48. Metuchen, N.J.: Scarecrow Press,
      1979.

The scientists whose lives, training, and careers form the basis of this study are the 504 women who were listed in the first three editions of American Men of Science. The author notes the encouragement provided by women's colleges, influence of the pioneer women scientists on their students, and the trend toward graduate education. Rossiter urges further research in this area.

494   ____. "'Women's Work' in Science, 1880-1910." Isis 71 (1980):381-98.
       An increase in the number of women seeking employment in scientific fields after 1880 coincided with changes in the structure of scientific work. This coincidence permitted unacknowledged sex segregation. Few women scientists became university teachers; instead they found careers as assistants in astronomy and in agricultural research in federal agencies. The new field of domestic science, established by women, remained a women's field. Other women educated as scientists entered academic administration as deans of women or became teachers of physical education.

495   ROTTIER, CATHERINE M. "Ellen Spencer Mussey and the Washington College of Law." Maryland Historical Magazine 69 (1974):361-82.
       Ellen Spencer Mussey and Emma Gillett founded the Washington School of Law in 1898. Rottier describes the history of this coeducational institution and Mussey's life. Mussey was also active in the National Association of Women Lawyers and a contributor to the Women Lawyers' Journal. (See also entry 420a.)

496   ROUSMANIERE, JOHN P. "Cultural Hybrid in the Slums: the College Woman and the Settlement House, 1889-94." American Quarterly 22 (1970):45-66.
       For women college graduates, settlement work was a satisfactory form of philanthropy. The settlement was a "middle-class outpost" where, according to this author, congenial colleagues shared a sense of superiority over other women.

497   RUBINOW, I. M. "The Problem of Domestic Service." Journal of Political Economy 14 (1906):502-19.
       Women preferred other occupations to domestic service because of the long hours, lack of independence, and low status of this work. Rubinow counted on technology to ease housekeeping tasks: "The genius who shall invent an automatic dishwasher and pot-scrubber will be the true benefactor of mankind."

498   SALMON, LUCY M. Domestic Service. New York and London: Macmillan, 1901. 307 pp.

This study of domestic service is frequently cited by
later writers. Recognizing that its low status makes this
occupation unattractive, Salmon recommends more democratic
treatment of servants, specialization and centralization
of some services, and graduate education in domestic science. Her comments on black and foreign-born servants
show her racist and ethnocentric assumptions: even children of immigrants are assumed not to understand American
ways.

499 _____. "Recent Progress in the Study of Domestic Service."
     Atlantic Monthly 96 (1905):628-35.
     A student of the problems of domestic service urges
     further investigation of training and working conditions.
     She also recommends that servants ally themselves with
     each other.

500 SANGER, MARGARET. Margaret Sanger: an Autobiography. New
     York: W. W. Norton, 1938. 504 pp.
     The leader of the birth-control movement began her
     career as a nurse in New York City. She witnessed the
     death of a young mother who had begged for a doctor's
     advice on how to prevent further pregnancies. This was
     the precipitating factor in her determination to make
     birth-control information and contraceptives generally
     available. See also the biography by David M. Kennedy,
     entry 438.

501 SANGSTER, MARGARET E. "Editorship as a Profession for Women."
     Forum (1895-96):445-55.
     Sangster encourages women to become newspaper and maga-
     zine editors. Although she emphasizes areas in which women
     can use their knowledge of homemaking and fashion, she does
     not exclude other possibilities. She suggests that this is
     fertile field for older women, and names some notable women
     editors.

501a SCUDDER, VIDA DUTTON. On Journey. New York: E. P. Dutton,
     1937. 445 pp.
     A teacher of English at Wellesley College from 1887
     until 1928, Vida Scudder was also a Christian Socialist,
     a founder of the College Settlements Association, and
     active in settlement work in Boston. Her autobiography
     is a chronicle not only of the events of her life but of
     her philosophical development.

502 SIMONS, MAY WOOD. Woman and the Social Problem. Chicago:
     Charles H. Kerr, 1899. 31 pp.
     This Socialist Party pamphlet links women's dependent
     position with capitalism, which uses working women against
     working men, limits their intellectual growth, and ruins

their health. Under socialism, women would be independent
whether they served society by raising children, by working
in the shop or factory, or by producing works of art.

503   SINCLAIR, ANDREW. The Better Half. New York: Harper & Row,
      1965. 401 pp.
         Although technology and urbanization furthered the cause
      of feminism, Sinclair finds the movement in many ways a
      failure. Although he has a tendency to generalize, the
      book is useful in setting feminism in its intellectual
      and social context.

504   SINCLAIR, UPTON. The Jungle. New York: Doubleday, 1906.
      413 pp.
         The famous novel about immigrant workers in Chicago's
      meatpacking industry includes a vivid picture of women
      working long hours, suffering harassment by bosses and by
      sudden layoffs, and trying to maintain family life with
      inadequate food and housing, filth, and constant risk of
      injury or illness.

505   SMITH, JUDITH E. "Our Own Kind: Family and Community Net-
      works in Providence." In A Heritage of Her Own, edited by
      Nancy F. Cott and Elizabeth H. Pleck, pp. 393-411. New
      York: Simon & Schuster, 1979.
         Patterns of life and work among Italian and Jewish immi-
      grants in Providence between 1880 and 1914 show that, in
      addition to household work, women contributed wages from
      home-work and factory work and income from boarders and
      lodgers.

506   SMUTS, ROBERT W. Women and Work in America. New York:
      Columbia University Press, 1959. 180 pp.
         This compact history traces the changes in women's
      place in the working world, beginning in 1890. Bibliography.

507   SOCHEN, JUNE. Movers and Shakers. New York: Quadrangle,
      1973. 320 pp.
         An introduction to feminist leaders of the twentieth
      century, including reformers, writers, and political
      figures.

508   _____. The New Woman: Feminism in Greenwich Village, 1910-
      1920. New York: Quadrangle, 1972. 175 pp.
         Sochen examines the lives, work, and thought of five
      women: Crystal Eastman, Henrietta Rodman, Ida Rauh, Neith
      Boyce, and Susan Glaspell. As rational and serious profes-
      sionals, they campaigned for change in the social structure
      and value system, seeing themselves not as isolated figures
      but as leaders of social change.

509   SOLTOW, MARTHA JANE, and WERY, MARY K. <u>American Women and</u>
      <u>the Labor Movement, 1825-1974: an Annotated Bibliography</u>.
      2d ed. Metuchen, N.J.: Scarecrow Press, 1976. 247 pp.
         This excellent bibliography includes publications on
      women in industrial work, their employment problems, and
      their participation in trade union organization. An appen-
      dix lists archives containing material related to women and
      labor. Subject, author, and cross-reference indexes.

509a SOPHIA SMITH COLLECTION. <u>Catalogs of the Sophia Smith Collec-</u>
      <u>tion, Women's History Archive, Smith College, Northampton,</u>
      <u>Massachusetts</u>. 7 vols. Boston: G. K. Hall, 1975.
         This catalogue of one of the major collections on women's
      history in the United States provides subject, author, and
      title entries for published works in the Smith College
      Library, as well as the manuscript and archival material
      in the Collection.

510   SPACKS, PATRICIA MEYER. "Selves in Hiding." In <u>Women's</u>
      <u>Autobiography: Essays in Criticism</u>, edited by Estelle C.
      Jelinek, pp. 112-32. Bloomington: Indiana University
      Press, 1980.
         Women's autobiographies reveal a kind of self-denial in
      the stories they tell about their private and public lives
      and in their estimation of the importance of their own work.
      Spacks studies the autobiographies of Emmeline Pankhurst,
      Dorothy Day, Emma Goldman, Eleanor Roosevelt, and Golda
      Meir; her observations are of interest to those who use
      autobiography as source material.

511   STEWART, WILLIAM RHINELANDER, ed. <u>The Philanthropic Work of</u>
      <u>Josephine Shaw Lowell</u>. New York: Macmillan, 1911. 584 pp.
         A brief biographical narrative connects a selection of
      Lowell's papers and letters. Widowed at twenty, she was a
      reformer active in the Charity Organization Society, the
      Consumers' League, and civil service reform. Glimpses of
      a hard-working, politically shrewd woman of principle make
      the reader wish for a more complete biography. A bibliog-
      raphy of Lowell's writings is included.

512   STRICKLAND, CHARLES E. "Juliette Low, the Girl Scouts, and
      the Role of American Women." In <u>Woman's Being, Woman's</u>
      <u>Place: Female Identity and Vocation in American History</u>,
      edited by Mary Kelley, pp. 252-64. Boston: G. K. Hall,
      1979.
         Brought up as a Southern lady, Juliette Low experienced
      a disastrous marriage. Determined that girls should be
      taught independence, she founded the Girl Scouts.

513   SUMNER, HELEN L. <u>History of Women in Industry in the United</u>
      <u>States</u>. United States Department of Labor, Report on

Condition of Woman and Child Wage-Earners in the United
States, vol. 9. Washington: U.S. Government Printing
Office, 1910. Reprint. New York: Arno Press, 1974.
277 pp.
   This essential source provides information about womens'
work, wages, and working conditions. It includes special
studies of the textile industry, clothing and sewing trades,
domestic service, food products, clerical work, and sales
work.

514   SUMNER, MARY BROWN. "The Spirit of the Strikers." Survey 23
      (January 22, 1910):550-55.
      A firsthand impression of the shirtwaist-makers' strike
      emphasizes the role played by Clara Lemlich.

515   SUTHERLAND, BRUCE. "Stella Miles Franklin's American Years."
      Meanjin Quarterly 24 (1965):439-54.
      The Australian author of My Brilliant Career came to
      Chicago in 1906 and became Margaret Dreier Robins's secre-
      tary. Within two years she was devoting all her time to
      the National Women's Trade Union League. She was active
      in the labor movement and wrote for the League's journal,
      Life and Labor. She left Chicago for London in 1915.

516   TALBOT, MARION, and ROSENBERRY, LOIS KIMBALL MATHEWS. The
      History of the American Association of University Women
      1881-1931. Boston: Houghton Mifflin, 1931. 479 pp.
      Founded in 1882 as the Association of Collegiate Alumnae
      under the leadership of Ellen H. Richards and Marion Talbot,
      the Association was intended to bring together women col-
      lege graduates. A major interest of the Association has
      been careers of women graduates. Beginning in 1907, it
      sponsored research and counseling to expand the vocational
      horizons of educated women and encourage them to enter
      fields other than teaching.

516a Tamiment Library. Catalog of the Tamiment Institute Library
      of New York University. 4 vols. Boston: G. K. Hall,
      1980.
      Originally the library of the Rand School, which existed
      from 1906 to 1956 to give New York City working people an
      opportunity for continuing education, the Tamiment Library
      became part of New York University in 1963. It is an ex-
      cellent collection of material on labor and the labor move-
      ment. The catalog includes books and pamphlets, with
      author, shelf list number, and subject access. Also in-
      cluded are indexes to the contents of the International
      Socialist Review (1900-18) and Mother Earth (1906-17).

517   TAX, MEREDITH. The Rising of the Women: Feminist Solidarity
      and Class Conflict, 1880-1917. New York and London:
      Monthly Review Press, 1980. 384 pp.

In spite of connections between the working-class struggle and the movement for women's liberation, no lasting
relationship developed. The author seeks the reasons for
this failure. She gives particular attention to the Women's
Trade Union League and the Illinois Woman's Alliance, and
to the Socialists and the IWW.

518   TENTLER, LESLIE WOODCOCK. Wage-Earning Women: Industrial
      Work and Family Life in the United States, 1900-1930.
      New York and Oxford: Oxford University Press, 1979.
      266 pp.
         The restriction of women to low-skill, poorly paid
      occupations reinforced the stereotype of inferiority and
      dependency in the world of work. Most unmarried women
      workers lived with their parents, accepted familial dis-
      cipline, and turned over their wages to their mothers.
      Women who lived on their own found it economically diffi-
      cult and socially isolated. Marriage offered security and
      a measure of authority within the home. Tentler believes
      this accounts for working-class women's lack of enthusiasm
      for the equal opportunity campaign, despite their need for
      economic independence. Bibliography.

519   TERRIS, VIRGINIA. Woman in America: A Guide to Information
      Sources. Detroit: Gale Research Co., 1980. 520 pp.
         This bibliography, broad in scope, is aimed at the gen-
      eral reader. It includes useful references on women's em-
      ployment, women in the arts, and sociology, as well as a
      section listing biographies and autobiographies. Arranged
      by subject, it has brief annotations and author, title, and
      subject indexes.

520   THOMAS, MARTHA CAREY. The Making of a Feminist: Early Jour-
      nals and Letters of M. Carey Thomas. Edited by Marjorie
      Housepian Dobkin. Kent, Ohio: Kent State University Press,
      1979. 314 pp.
         Although these selections end in 1884 when Thomas was
      appointed Dean of the Faculty at Bryn Mawr, they reveal
      much about the girlhood and young womanhood of a major
      figure in women's education, and about the conditions of
      higher education, which she did much to change.

521   THWING, C. F. "What Becomes of College Women." North American
      Review 161 (1895):546-53.
         The author found college graduates pursuing a variety of
      occupations, including teaching. He was surprised to dis-
      cover that few distinguished women writers were graduates.
      The evidence, he believes, proves that college education
      for women is worthwhile.

108

522 TOBEMKIN, ELIAS. "The Immigrant Girl in Chicago." Survey 23
      (1909-10):189-95.
          Immigrant working girls resisted union organizing; the
      author believes that they did not want to acknowledge pub-
      licly their status as workers.

523 TRUE, RUTH S. The Neglected Girl. New York: Survey Asso-
      ciates, 1914. Reprinted in West Side Studies. College
      Park, Md.: McGrath Publishing Co., 1969. 143 pp.
          In a social center for girls on New York's West Side,
      settlement workers learned about the lives of girls from
      Irish and Italian families. The girls worked in factories
      and were likely to marry very young. Many of their mothers
      performed janitorial or laundry work to add to the family
      income.

524 UNITED STATES. CONGRESS. SENATE. Report on Condition of
      Woman and Child Wage-Earners in the United States. 19 vols.
      61st Congress. 2d Session. Senate Document nos. 86-104.
      Washington, D.C.: U.S. Government Printing Office, 1912.
          The report prepared by the Labor Department consists of
      nineteen studies of industries that employ women and chil-
      dren, trade unions, health of women and children workers,
      and legislation. This is a rich source of information.
      The historical volume by Helen Sumner has been reprinted
      (see entry 513).

525 UNITED STATES. DEPARTMENT OF AGRICULTURE. Report No. 103.
      Social and Labor Needs of Farm Women. Washington, D.C.:
      U.S. Government Printing Office, 1915. 100 pp.
      _____. _____. Report No. 104. Domestic Needs of Farm Women.
      Washington, D.C.: U.S. Government Printing Office, 1915.
      100 pp.
      _____. _____. Report No. 106. Economic Needs of Farm Women.
      Washington, D.C.: U.S. Government Printing Office, 1915.
      100 pp.
          In 1913 the Secretary of Agriculture sent letters to
      55,000 farm women asking their suggestions for ways in
      which the Department could serve them. These reports con-
      sist chiefly of quotations from their replies. Their prob-
      lems--many of them related to the remoteness of their
      farms--emerge vividly in these letters.

526 VAN KLEECK, MARY. Artificial Flower Makers. New York:
      Survey Associates, 1913. 261 pp.
          The Committee on Women's Work of the Russell Sage Foun-
      dation sponsored a series of studies of women's trades in
      New York City. Artificial-flower making was selected be-
      cause it illustrated problems common to a number of indus-
      tries (home-work, child labor, and seasonal unemployment)
      and the information gathered could be applied to other

trades and other cities. Investigators visited the workers' homes as well as the factories and collected data on their backgrounds, working conditions, wages, hours, and opportunities to learn the trade.

527   _____. Women in the Bookbinding Trade. New York: Survey Associates, 1913. 270 pp.
        One of a series of studies of women's occupations sponsored by the Russell Sage Foundation, this gives a detailed description of women's jobs, hours, and training in bookbinding. Illustrated with photographs by Lewis Hine.

528   _____. Working Girls in Evening Schools. New York: Survey Associates, 1914. 252 pp.
        In a study sponsored by the Russell Sage Foundation, Van Kleeck surveyed some 13,000 girls enrolled in evening classes, gathering information about their occupations, hours of work, nationality, and previous schooling. She recommends increased attention to occupational training and to the great variety of occupations at which young women worked.

529   VAN VORST, BESSIE, and VAN VORST, MARIE. The Woman Who Toils. New York: Doubleday, Page, 1903. 303 pp.
        Two well-to-do women record their experiences as workers in Pittsburgh, Chicago, and New York State and their observations of working girls and how they lived. They conclude that girls who work only for spending money should not be in competition with those who must work for a living, and recommend training in appropriately feminine crafts for the first group.

530   VAN VORST, MARIE. Amanda of the Mill. New York: Dodd-Mead, 1905. 340 pp.
        In the context of a passionate tale about a Southern mountain girl who falls in love with an elegant but alcoholic labor leader, the author conveys a vivid picture of life in and around the textile mills of the South. Amanda is discovered by the mill-owner's wife and taken North for education and refining, but returns to help the cause of her poor brothers and sisters.

530a   Vocations for the Trained Woman. Opportunities Other Than Teaching, Introductory Papers, vol. 1, edited by Agnes F. Perkins. 296 pp. Agriculture, Social Services, Secretarial Service, Business of Real Estate, vol. 2, edited by Eleanor Martin and Margaret A. Post. 175 pp. Boston: Women's Educational and Industrial Union, 1910, 1914.
        The first volume contains brief essays by experts on a wide variety of occupations for educated women, from advertising and interior decoration to clerical work to forestry.

Prospects for success are evaluated. Volume 2 offers
longer, more detailed studies (including regional information) of the fields listed in its title.

531   WALD, LILLIAN D. The House on Henry Street. New York:
Henry Holt & Co., 1915. 316 pp.
      The founder of the Henry Street Settlement describes in
anecdotal style her experiences in nursing and settlement
work in New York's Lower East Side.

532   WEIGLEY, EMMA SEIFRIT. "It Might Have Been Euthenics: the
Lake Placid Conferences and the Home Economics Movement."
American Quarterly 26 (1974):79-96.
      The idea of home economics as a discipline and the pro-
fession of home economist developed through a series of
conferences at Lake Placid 1898-1909. The culmination of
the conferences was the founding of the American Home Economics Association.

533   _____. Sarah Tyson Rorer, the Nation's Instructress in Dietet-
ics and Cookery. Memoirs of The American Philosophical
Society, vol. 119. Philadelphia: The American Philosophical Society, 1977. 196 pp.
      To alleviate boredom, Mrs. Rorer, a sickly housewife,
took up cooking and became a nationally known figure in
the field. She presided over the Philadelphia Cooking
School for twenty years, advocating a simpler diet and more
efficient kitchens. She developed special invalid diets
and instructed nurses and doctors in the elements of invalid nutrition. With very little personal documentation
available, Weigley has presented an interesting and tanta-
lizing biography.

534   WELLS, ANNA MARY. Miss Marks and Miss Woolley. Boston:
Houghton Mifflin, 1978. 268 pp.
      Mary E. Woolley was president of Mount Holyoke College
from 1901 until 1937. Her intimate friend, Jeanette Marks,
taught English and shared the president's house. This dual
biography examines the careers and relationship of two women
of strong personality and ambition.

535   WELLS, MILDRED WHITE. Unity in Diversity: the History of the
General Federation of Women's Clubs. Washington, D.C.:
General Federation of Women's Clubs, 1953. 525 pp.
      An official history of the Federation, this provides
biographies of its presidents as well as information on
organization, national meetings, and programs. Many of
the presidents before 1914 were professional women
(Sorosis, an organization of professional women, was important in the founding of the Federation.) See Karen J.
Blair, The Clubwoman as Feminist, entry 350.

536 WELTER, BARBARA. "The Cult of True Womanhood." American
     Quarterly 18 (1966):151-74.
          Domestic skills, piety, purity, and passivity marked
     the True Woman, whose image Welter draws from women's maga-
     zines, religious tracts, and other sources. Her place was
     at home, under the protection of her husband. Yet, as
     Welter points out, True Womanhood had a flaw: if women
     were so nearly perfect, they should participate in running
     the world. This article has influenced subsequent
     scholarship.

537 WERTHEIMER, BARBARA MAYER. We Were There: the Story of Work-
     ing Women in America. New York: Pantheon, 1977. 427 pp.
          This survey of working women from the seventeenth cen-
     tury until 1914 is an excellent introduction to the Women's
     Trade Union League, women in trade unions, the Triangle
     fire, and many individuals in the labor movement.
     Bibliography.

538 WHARTON, EDITH NEWBOLD. A Backward Glance. New York and
     London: D. Appleton-Century Co., 1934. 385 pp.
          The novelist's autobiography gives a charming account
     of her travels and her famous friends, particularly Henry
     James, as well as evidence of her devotion to her work.
     The standard biography is R. W. B. Lewis, Edith Wharton,
     a Biography (New York: Harper & Row, 1975).

539 _____. The House of Mirth. London and New York: Macmillan,
     1905. 516 pp.
          This is a brilliant portrayal of the plight of a woman
     of good family without money. No work is appropriate for
     Lily Bart, yet she must keep up the appearance of living
     elegantly. In the New York social world in which she moves,
     marriage is the only acceptable means of support for a young
     woman of her position.

539a WILLARD, FRANCES E. Occupations for Women. New York: The
     Success Company, 1897. 504 pp.
          Willard's essays, intended for educated middle-class
     women, give examples of women who have succeeded in each
     occupation, as well as general advice on behavior, dress,
     and training.

540 WILLETT, MAUD HURD. The Employment of Women in the Clothing
     Trade. New York: Columbia University Press, 1902. 206 pp.
          This analysis of women's work in all branches of New
     York City's garment industry gives attention to wages,
     hours, working conditions, trade unions, and variations
     according to ethnic group.

541 WILSON, MARGARET GIBBONS. The American Woman in Transition:
     the Urban Influence, 1870-1920. Westport, Conn. and
     London: Greenwood Press, 1979. 252 pp.
         Changes in American urban life in the late nineteenth
     and early twentieth centuries affected the lives of middle-
     class women, making it possible for them to move out of a
     strictly home-centered existence. Wilson examines the
     effect of improved public transportation, availability of
     boarding houses and apartments, women's clubs, light manu-
     facturing industries and the boom in white-collar jobs, as
     well as the increasing rate of divorce and the decreasing
     number of children. She provides much statistical informa-
     tion to support her conclusions. Bibliography.

542 WILSON, OTTO. Life of Dr. Kate Waller Barrett. In Fifty
     Years' Work With Girls, Otto Wilson, pp. 139-203.
     Alexandria, Va.: The National Florence Crittenton Mission,
     1933. Reprinted with Kate Waller Barrett. Some Practical
     Suggestions on the Conduct of a Rescue Home. New York:
     Arno Press, 1974.
         As a young minister's wife in Richmond, Virginia, Kate
     Waller Barrett became concerned with the plight of unmar-
     ried mothers and the need for rescue homes for them. She
     worked with Charles Crittenton to establish the Florence
     Crittenton missions and after his death became president
     of the organization. She served as president of the Na-
     tional Council of Women. This adulatory memorial suggests
     an interesting, energetic, and political woman.

543 WINSTON, ELIZABETH. "The Autobiographer and Her Readers:
     From Apology to Affirmation." In Women's Autobiography:
     Essays in Criticism, edited by Estelle C. Jelinek, pp. 93-
     111. Bloomington: Indiana University Press, 1980.
         Before 1920, women autobiographers defended themselves
     against criticism for neglecting their home and family re-
     sponsibilities in pursuit of their work. Examples in this
     review of literary women's autobiographies include Charlotte
     Perkins Gilman, Elizabeth Haldane, and Edith Wharton.

544 WOLFE, ALLIS ROSENBERG. "Women, Consumerism, and the National
     Consumers' League in the Progressive Era, 1900-1923."
     Labor History 16 (1975):378-92.
         Most of the members of the Consumers' League were women
     of the upper and middle classes. Under the leadership of
     Florence Kelley, the League campaigned for protective legis-
     lation and ethical control of consumption. The Consumers'
     Label attached to approved products was their major weapon.
     The League never succeeded in crossing the class barrier;
     when the ILGWU Union label supplanted the Consumers' Label,
     the organization lost its strong public image.

545   WOMEN'S EDUCATIONAL AND INDUSTRIAL UNION. Department of
Research. The Living Wage of Women Workers: A Study of
Incomes and Expenditures of 450 Women in the City of Boston.
Studies in Economic Relations of Women, vol. 3. London:
Longmans Green & Co., 1911. 90 pp.
    This is a useful source of detailed information on how
working women lived and spent their wages.

546   WOOD, MARY I. The History of the General Federation. New
York: General Federation of Women's Clubs, 1914. 445 pp.
    An early account of the history of the General Federa-
tion of Women's Clubs, this describes its first twenty-two
years. See Mildred White Wells, Unity in Diversity (1953),
entry 535.

547   WOODS, ROBERT A., and KENNEDY, ALBERT J., eds. Young Working
Girls: a Summary of Evidence from Two Thousand Social
Workers. Boston: Houghton Mifflin, 1913. 185 pp.
    The National Federation of Settlements collected data
from settlement workers on girls between the ages of four-
teen and eighteen: their entrance into the job market,
training, vocational counseling, recreational activities,
family life, and morality. Suggestions for settlement
house programs are offered, based on the results of the
survey.

548   WRIGHT, CARROLL D. "Are Women Hurting the Chances of Men in
Business?" Chautauquan 26 (1897-98):79-83.
    Examining the censuses of 1879, 1880, and 1890, and the
Department of Labor report, "Work and Wages of Men, Women,
and Children," the author concludes that women are indeed
competing with men in a variety of fields including clerical occupations, journalism, art, and music. In manufacturing, however, women are replacing children. He predicts
that in time women will receive equal pay with men for the
same work.

549   YANS-McLAUGHLIN, CONSTANCE. Family and Community: Italian
Immigrants in Buffalo 1880-1930. Ithaca, N.Y. and London:
Cornell University Press, 1977. 286 pp.
    Italian families in Buffalo accepted certain kinds of
women's work as appropriate under certain conditions.
Women were employed in the canning industry, and some took
lodgers. The author explains this in terms of their socio-
cultural background.

Author Index

Author Index

Title Index

Subject Index

Copyediting directed by Ara Salibian
Text formatted and produced by Diane Dillon
Camera-ready copy typed by Jan Pinette
    on an IBM Selectric
Printed on 60# Warren's "66," an acid-free paper,
    and bound by Braun-Brumfield, Inc.
    of Ann Arbor, Michigan.